Lone Pine Publishing

# Annuals
## *for* OHIO

*Debra Knapke*
*Alison Beck*

© 2003 by Lone Pine Publishing
First printed in 2003   10 9 8 7 6 5 4 3 2 1
Printed in Canada

**The Publisher: Lone Pine Publishing**

10145 – 81 Avenue                         1808 – B Street NW, Suite 140
Edmonton, AB, Canada T6E 1W9              Auburn, WA, USA 98001
Website: www.lonepinepublishing.com

**National Library of Canada Cataloguing in Publication Data**

Knapke, Debra, 1955–
    Annuals for Ohio / Debra Knapke and Alison Beck.

    Includes index.
    ISBN 1-55105-388-8

    1. Annuals (Plants)—Ohio. 2. Gardening—Ohio. I. Beck, Alison,
1971–  II. Title.
SB422.K52 2003          635.9'312'09771          C2003-910555-5

*Editorial Director:* Nancy Foulds
*Project Editor:* Shelagh Kubish
*Editorial:* Shelagh Kubish, Dawn Loewen
*Illustrations Coordinator:* Carol Woo
*Photo Editor:* Don Williamson
*Production Manager:* Gene Longson
*Book Design & Layout:* Heather Markham
*Cover Design:* Gerry Dotto
*Production Support:* Ian Dawe, Jeff Fedorkiw
*Scanning, Separations & Film:* Elite Lithographers Co.

*Photography:* all photos by Tim Matheson or Tamara Eder except All-America Selections 88a, 231b, 237b; Doris Baucom 233b; Joan de Grey 177a; Elliot Engley 26b, 29, 30a,b,c,d&e, EuroAmerican 77a&b, 125a&b, 144, 160a, 191b, 232, 233a, 281b; Anne Gordon 228; Horticolor (91 10 51) 113, (N1503018) 112, (G450005) 280b; Horticultural Photography: Arthur Orans 123b; Debra Knapke 65b, 66b, 67a, 95a&b, 165a&b, 176, 177b, 229a; Colin Laroque 10; Janet Loughrey 122, 123a, 221b, 229b; Kim Patrick O'Leary 12b, 26c, 27a, 65a, 80a, 94, 132a, 141a&b, 142, 145b, 147a, 151a, 169a&b, 182, 183a&b, 205b, 245a, 267a; Allison Penko 110b; Robert Ritchie 43b, 45; Peter Thompstone 19, 61a&b, 136, 137a, 151b, 179a, 180a&b, 239a, 257b.

*Cover photos:* by Tim Matheson, fuchsia, sunflower, dahlia, gazania; by Tamara Eder, Mexican sunflower

*Map:* frost-date data from National Oceanic and Atmospheric Administration National Climatic Data Center, Asheville, North Carolina

We acknowledge the financial support of the Government of Canada through the Book Publishing Industry Development Program (BPIDP) for our publishing activities.

PC: P1

# CONTENTS

# ACKNOWLEDGMENTS

We gratefully acknowledge all who were involved in this project, as well as the many gorgeous public and private gardens that provided the setting for photographs in this book. Special thanks are extended to the following individuals and organizations: Barbara and Douglas Bloom, Thea and Don Bloomquist, Heidi Clausen, Robert Ritchie, Peter Thompstone, Agriculture Canada Central Experimental Farm, Bordine Nursery, Casa Loma Gardens, Chicago Botanic Gardens, Cranbrook Gardens, Cranbrook Garden Auxiliary, Cullen Gardens, Edwards Gardens, Inniswood Metro Gardens, Montreal Botanic Garden, Morton Arboretum, Niagara Parks Botanical Gardens and Royal Botanical Gardens.

I am extremely grateful to all the teachers, writers, horticulturists, botanists, photographers, gardeners and friends who have taught, guided and otherwise influenced me over the years. I wish to especially thank Steven Still; Denise Adams; Fred Hower; Chris Baker; my husband, Tony; and our children, Sarah, John and Robert. —*Debra Knapke*

# THE FLOWERS AT A GLANCE

A PICTORIAL GUIDE IN ALPHABETICAL ORDER, BY COMMON NAME

Abutilon
p. 48

African daisy
p. 50

Ageratum
p. 52

Alyssum
p. 56

Amaranth
p. 58

Baby blue-eyes
p. 70

Anagallis
p. 62

Angel's trumpet
p. 64

Angelonia
p. 68

Bachelor's button
p. 74

Bacopa
p. 76

Bells-of-Ireland
p. 82

Begonia
p. 78

Bidens
p. 84

Black-eyed Susan
p. 86

Black-eyed Susan vine
p. 90

Blanket flower
p. 92

Blood flower
p. 94

Browallia
p. 96

Calendula
p. 98

California poppy
p. 100

Candytuft
p. 102

Canterbury bells
p. 104

Cape marigold
p. 106

Celosia
p. 108

Chilean glory flower
p. 112

China aster
p. 114

Chinese forget-me-not
p. 116

Climbing snapdragon
p. 122

Cleome
p. 118

Coleus
p. 124

Coreopsis
p. 128

Cosmos
p. 130

Creeping zinnia
p. 134

Cup flower
p. 136

Dahlberg daisy
p. 138

Dahlia
p. 140

Diascia
p. 144

Dusty miller
p. 146

Dwarf morning glory
p. 148

Flowering flax
p. 154

Fan flower
p. 150

Felicia
p. 152

Four-o'clock flower
p. 156

Fuchsia
p. 158

Gazania
p. 162

Geranium
p. 164

Globe amaranth
p. 168

Godetia
p. 170

Heliotrope
p. 172

Impatiens
p. 178

Lantana
p. 182

Larkspur
p. 184

Hyacinth bean
p. 176

Lavatera
p. 186

Licorice plant
p. 190

Lisianthus
p. 192

Livingstone daisy
p. 194

Mexican sunflower
p. 204

Lobelia
p. 196

Love-in-a-mist
p. 198

Marigold
p. 200

Million bells
p. 206

Monkey flower
p. 208

Morning glory
p. 210

Moss rose
p. 214

Nasturtium
p. 216

Nemesia
p. 220

Nicotiana
p. 222

Painted-tongue
p. 226

Passion flower
p. 228

Periwinkle
p. 230

Persian shield
p. 232

Petunia
p. 234

Phlox
p. 238

Poppy
p. 240

Sage
p. 244

Scabiosa
p. 248

Strawflower
p. 258

Snapdragon
p. 250

Statice
p. 254

Stock
p. 256

Sunflower
p. 260

Swan River daisy
p. 262

Sweet pea
p. 264

Verbena
p. 266

Viola
p. 270

Wishbone flower
p. 274

Zinnia
p. 276

# INTRODUCTION

True annuals are plants that germinate, mature, bloom, set seed and die in one growing season. The plants we treat as annuals, or bedding plants, may be annuals, biennials or tender perennials. Our expectation is to plant them in the spring or summer and enjoy them for only one growing season. Many biennials, if started early enough, will flower the year you plant them, and many plants that are perennial in warmer climates will grow and flower before they succumb to our cold winter temperatures.

Annuals provide long-lasting color and fill in spaces in garden beds. Most annuals are started indoors and then transplanted into the garden after the last spring frost, but some can be sown directly in the garden. A sure sign of spring's arrival is the rush of gardeners to local garden centers, greenhouses and farmers' markets to pick out their new annuals.

The climate in Ohio is excellent for growing most annuals. Summer weather offers warm days and nights and, frequently, high humidity. Annuals that love these conditions thrive in the heat, but they aren't as likely to be burned out by summer's end as they would be in the southern U.S., where the heat is far greater. The downside to all this warm weather is that annuals that prefer cool summer weather don't do as well in Ohio and tend to die back over the hottest part of the season. Keeping them well watered and out of the full sun will often encourage them to revive as cooler fall weather sets in.

In Ohio the last spring frost occurs anywhere from mid- to late April (see map, p. 13), and the first fall frost generally comes in October. Ohio gardeners can expect a frost-free period of about five months, which gives annuals plenty of time to mature and fill the garden with abundant color. If a specific spring or fall is warmer than usual, gardeners can make additional plantings and enjoy annuals a little longer. Flowers that tend to fade in excessive heat can be planted in early spring and enjoyed until the summer heat causes them to die back. Make a

sowing of these same frost-tolerant plants in August, and they will thrive in the cooler weather of fall.

Rainfall is fairly dependable in Ohio, and with good mulch to prevent water loss, most plants will usually need very little supplemental watering. In a dry year, however, Ohio may receive no significant rainfall from July through early September. In these years supplemental watering will be necessary.

Annuals are popular because they produce lots of flowers, in a wide variety of colors, over a long period of time. Many annuals bloom continually from spring right through to early fall. Beyond this basic appeal, gardeners are constantly finding new ways to include annuals in their gardens, using them to accent areas in an established border, featuring them as the main attraction in a new garden or combining them with trees, shrubs, perennials and even vegetables. Many annuals are adapted to a variety of growing conditions, from hot, dry sun to cool, damp shade. They are fun for beginners and experienced gardeners alike and, because annuals are temporary and relatively inexpensive, they can be easily replaced if they are undesirable or past their prime.

Some of the most popular, easy to grow and reliable annuals include geraniums, petunias, impatiens and marigolds, but the selection of annuals is increasing every year. New species have been introduced from other parts of the world. There are new and sometimes improved varieties of old favorites with expanded color ranges or increased pest resistance. With the increased interest in organic gardening, and in response to concerns about overhybridization, the use of native plants and heritage varieties is on the upswing.

Some new varieties may experience a short period of popularity, but, failing to meet the expectations of the gardening public, fall by the wayside. Others join the ranks of the favorites. Greatly improved varieties that have been tried in gardens across the United States and Canada may be judged by members of the horticultural industry 'All-America Selections Winners.' These outstanding plants are the most widely known and frequently grown. They usually carry the AASW seal and are worth seeking out.

## Average Last-Frost Date

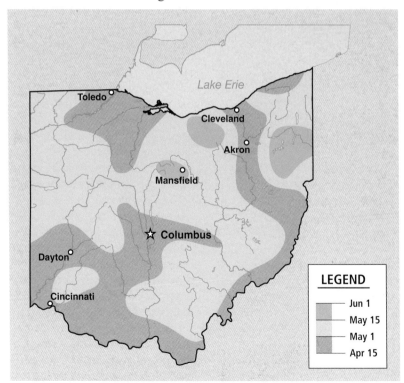

Toledo

Lake Erie

Cleveland

Akron

Mansfield

☆ Columbus

Dayton

Cincinnati

**LEGEND**

Jun 1
May 15
May 1
Apr 15

# ANNUAL GARDENS

The short life of annuals allows gardeners flexibility and freedom when planning a garden. Where trees and shrubs form the permanent structure or the 'bones' of the garden, and perennials and groundcovers fill the spaces between them, annuals add bold patterns and bright splashes of color. Include annuals anywhere you would like some variety and dazzle—in pots staggered up porch steps or on a deck, in windowsill planters or in hanging baskets. Even well-established gardens are brightened and given a new look with the addition of annual flowers.

Something as simple as a planting of impatiens under a tree can be different each year with different varieties and color combinations. When planning your garden, consult as many sources as you can. Look through gardening books and ask friends and greenhouse experts for advice. Notice what you like or dislike about various gardens, and make a list of the plants you would like to include in your garden.

You can create whatever style garden you desire by cleverly mixing annuals. A tidy, symmetrical, formal garden can be enhanced by adding only a few types of annuals or by choosing annuals of the same flower color. In the same garden, adding many different species and colors of annuals would relax the neat plantings of trees and shrubs. An informal, cottage-style garden can be a riot of plants and colors.

When choosing annuals, most people make the color, size and shape of the flowers their prime considerations. Other aspects to consider are

Coleus

Sweet potato vine

the size and shape of the plant and leaves. A variety of flower, plant and leaf sizes, shapes and colors will make your garden more interesting. Consult the individual plant entries and the Quick Reference Chart on p. 282.

Colors have different effects on our senses. Cool colors, such as purple, blue and green, are soothing and relaxing and can make a small garden appear larger. Some annuals with cool colors are lobelia, ageratum and browallia. Warm colors, such as red, orange and yellow, are more stimulating and appear to fill larger spaces. Warm colors can make even the largest, most imposing garden seem warm and welcoming. Annuals with warm colors include calendula and celosia.

If you have time to enjoy your garden mainly in the evenings, you may want to consider pale colors such as white and yellow. These show up well at dusk and even at night. Some plants, such as moonflower (one of the morning glories) have flowers that open only in the evenings and often have fragrant blossoms that add an attractive dimension to the evening garden.

Foliage color varies a great deal as well. Some annuals are grown for their interesting or colorful foliage and not for the flowers at all, yet some plants have interesting foliage and flowers. Leaves come in almost every imaginable shade of green and also in a range of other colors including red, purple, yellow, blue and bronze. Some foliage is variegated, that is, patterned or with veins that contrast with the color of the leaves. Some foliage plants, such as coleus, are used by themselves, while others, such as dusty miller, provide an interesting backdrop for brightly colored flowers.

## ANNUALS WITH INTERESTING FOLIAGE

Amaranth 'Illumination'
Begonia
Coleus
Licorice Plant
Nasturtium
Persian Shield
Sweet Potato Vine

Texture is another important element to consider. Both foliage and flowers have a visual texture. Large leaves appear coarse in texture and can make a garden appear smaller and more shaded. Coarse-textured flowers appear bold and dramatic and can be seen from far away. Small leaves appear fine in texture and create a sense of increased space and light. Fine-textured flowers appear soothing. Sometimes the flowers and foliage of a plant have contrasting textures. Using a variety of textures helps make a garden interesting and appealing.

## FINE-TEXTURED ANNUALS

Alyssum
Bacopa
Dahlberg Daisy
Larkspur
Lobelia
Love-in-a-Mist
Swan River Daisy

Dahlberg daisy

## COARSE-TEXTURED ANNUALS

Cleome
Mexican Sunflower
Nicotiana
Scented Geranium
Sunflower
Sweet Potato Vine

Sunflower

Nicotiana

# Getting Started

Before you start shopping for or planting your annuals, consider the growing conditions in each area of your garden. For your plants to thrive, it's important that their specific needs be coordinated with the microenvironments in your garden. Plants will be healthier and less susceptible to problems if grown in their preferred conditions. It is difficult to significantly modify your garden's existing conditions; match the plants to the garden instead. Consult the individual plant entries and the Quick Reference Chart on p. 282.

The levels of light, the porosity, pH and texture of soil, the amount of exposure in your garden and the plants' tolerance to frost provide guidelines for selecting your plants. Sketching your garden will help you visualize the various conditions. Note any shaded, low-lying, wet, exposed or windy areas. Understanding your garden's growing conditions will help you learn to recognize which plants will perform best, saving you money and time. Conversely, experimenting with different annuals will help you learn about the conditions of your garden.

## Light

Four levels of light may be present in a garden: full sun, partial shade (partial sun), light shade and full shade. Available light is affected by buildings, trees, fences and the position of the

Amaranth

ground underneath a small-leaved tree, such as a birch, is often lightly shaded. **Full shade** locations, which would include the north side of a house, receive no direct sunlight.

Sun-loving plants may become tall and straggly and flower poorly in too much shade. Shade-loving plants may get scorched leaves or even wilt and die if they get too much sun. Many other plants tolerate a wide range of light conditions.

## ANNUALS FOR SUN
Amaranth
Celosia
Cosmos
Geranium
Globe Amaranth
Heliotrope
Marigold
Moss Rose
Sage
Statice

sun at different times of the day and year. Knowing what light is available in your garden will help you determine where to place each plant.

Plants in **full sun** locations, such as along south-facing walls, receive direct sunlight for six or more hours a day. **Partial shade** locations, such as east- or west-facing walls, receive direct sunlight for part of the day and shade for the rest. **Light shade** locations receive shade for most or all of the day, but some light filters through to ground level. For example, the

## ANNUALS FOR SHADE
Browallia
Canterbury Bells
Godetia
Impatiens
Nicotiana
Viola

Impatiens

## ANNUALS FOR ANY LIGHT
Black-eyed Susan
Coleus
Cup Flower
Fan Flower
Lobelia
Nasturtium
New Guinea Impatiens
Wax Begonia

# Soil

Good soil is an extremely important element of a healthy garden. Plant roots rely on the air, water and nutrients that are held within soil. Plants also depend on soil to hold them upright. The soil, in turn, benefits in at least three ways: plant roots improve soil texture by breaking down large particles; plants prevent soil erosion by reducing the amount of exposed surface and by binding together small particles with their roots; and plants increase soil fertility when they die and break down, adding organic nutrients to the soil and feeding beneficial microorganisms.

Soil is made up of particles of different sizes. Sand particles are the largest. Water drains quickly from sandy soil and nutrients tend to get washed away. Sandy soil does not compact very easily because the large particles leave air pockets between them. Clay particles, which are the smallest, can be seen only through a microscope. Clay holds the most nutrients, but it also compacts easily and has little air space. Clay is slow to absorb water and equally slow to let it drain. Silt is midway in size between sand and clay. Most soils are composed of a combination of these different particle sizes and are called loams.

Fan flower with impatiens

It is important to consider the pH level (acidity or alkalinity) of soil, which influences the availability of nutrients. Most plants thrive in soil with a pH between 5.5 and 7.5. Soil pH varies a great deal from place to place in Ohio. Kits for testing the pH of soil can be purchased at most garden centers. There are also soil-testing labs that can fully analyze the pH as well as the quantities of various nutrients in your soil. The acidity of soil can be reduced by adding horticultural lime or wood ashes and increased by adding sulfur, peat moss, pine needles or chopped oak leaves. If you are trying to grow plants that require soil with a pH quite different than that in your garden, consider growing them in a planter or raised

## ANNUALS FOR MOIST SOIL
Cleome
Lavatera
Monkey Flower
Viola

## ANNUALS FOR DRY SOIL
Cape Marigold
Cosmos
Livingstone Daisy
Marigold
Moss Rose

bed where it is easier to control and alter the pH level of soil.

Drainage, the ability of water to move through soil, is affected by soil type and terrain in your garden. Gravelly soil on a hillside will drain very quickly, while low-lying areas may drain very slowly, if at all. Water retention can be improved by adding organic matter. Drainage may be improved in wet areas by installing a drainage system, by adding sand or gravel or by building raised beds.

Monkey flower (above), Livingstone daisy (below)

## Exposure
Your garden is exposed to wind, heat, cold and rain, and some plants are better adapted than others to withstand the potential damage of these forces. Buildings, walls, fences, hills, hedges, trees and even tall perennials influence and often reduce exposure.

Wind and heat are the most likely elements to damage annuals. The sun can be very intense, and heat can rise quickly on a sunny afternoon. Plant annuals that tolerate or even thrive in hot weather in the hot spots in your garden.

Moss-lined hanging baskets are especially susceptible to wind and heat exposure, losing water from the soil surface and the leaves. Water can evaporate from all sides of a moss basket, and in hot or windy locations moisture can be depleted very quickly. Hanging baskets look wonderful, but watch for wilting, and water the baskets regularly to keep them looking great.

Overwatering or too much rain can also be damaging. Early in the season, seeds or seedlings can be washed away in heavy rain; mulch around the seeded area will help prevent this problem. Established annuals, or their flowers, can be beaten down by heavy rain. Most annuals will recover, but some, such as petunias, are slow to do so. Place sensitive annuals in protected areas, or choose plants or varieties that are quick to recover from rain damage. Many of the small-flowered petunia varieties now available are quick to recover from heavy rain.

## Frost Tolerance

When planting annuals, consider their ability to tolerate an unexpected frost. The dates for last frost and first frost vary greatly from region to region in North America. Most Ohio gardeners can expect a chance of frost until mid- to late April. The map on p. 13 gives a general idea of when you can expect your last frost. Keep in mind that these dates can vary significantly from year to year and within the general regions. Your local garden center should be able to provide more

precise information on frost expectations for your area.

Annuals are grouped into three categories based on how they tolerate cold weather: hardy, half-hardy or tender. Consult the Quick Reference Chart on p. 282 for hardiness categories of annuals in this book.

**Hardy** annuals can tolerate low temperatures and even frost. They can be planted in the garden early and may continue to flower long into fall or even winter. I had hardy violas planted close to the house and they continued to flower even after a snowfall covered them. Many hardy annuals are sown directly in the garden before the last frost date.

**Half-hardy** annuals can tolerate a light frost but will be killed by a heavy one. These annuals, generally started early from seed indoors, can be planted out around the last-frost date.

Johnny-jump-up

**Tender** annuals have no frost tolerance at all and might suffer if the temperatures drop to a few degrees above freezing. For example, nasturtiums become a soggy mess after a light frost. Tender plants are often started early indoors and not planted in the garden until the last-frost date has passed and the ground has had a chance to warm up. The advantage to these annuals is that they often tolerate hot summer temperatures.

Protecting plants from frost is relatively simple. Plants can be covered overnight with sheets, towels, burlap or even cardboard boxes. Don't use plastic because it doesn't retain heat and therefore doesn't provide plants with any insulation.

Marigold

Nasturtium

# PREPARING THE GARDEN

Taking the time to properly prepare your flowerbeds will save you time and effort over the summer. Give your annuals a good start with weeded soil that has had organic material added. For container gardens, use potting soil because regular garden soil loses its structure when used in pots, quickly compacting into a solid mass that drains poorly.

Loosen the soil with a large garden fork and remove the weeds. Avoid working the soil when it is very wet or very dry because you will damage the soil structure by breaking down the pockets that hold air and water.

Organic matter is an important component of soil. It increases the water-holding and nutrient-holding capacity of sandy soil and binds together the large particles. It increases the water-absorbing and draining potential of clay soil by opening up spaces between the tiny particles. Common organic additives for your soil include grass clippings, shredded leaves, peat moss, chopped straw, well-rotted manure and composted bark.

When preparing an area for planting, it is advisable to add a 3–4" layer of organic matter and work it into the soil with a spade or rototiller. To determine how much organic matter you need to provide a 3–4" layer, use the following equation:

Compute area by multiplying length of garden bed by width (for example, 6' × 18' = 108 sq. ft.).

Multiply area by inches of depth wanted (108 sq. ft. × 4" = 432 sq. ft.).

Divide by 12 to get the amount in cu. ft. (432 ÷ 12 = 36 cu. ft.).

Because 27 cu. ft. equals 1 cu. yd., you would need 1$\frac{1}{3}$ cu. yd. of organic matter to provide a 4" layer to an area of 108 sq. ft.

## Composting

Any organic matter you add will be of greater benefit to your soil if it has been composted first. In natural environments, such as forests or meadows, compost is created when leaves, plant bits and other debris are broken down on the soil surface. This process will also take place in your garden beds if you work fresh organic matter into the soil. However, microorganisms that break down organic matter use the same nutrients as your plants. The tougher the organic matter, the more

nutrients in the soil will be used trying to break the matter down. As a result, your plants will be robbed of vital nutrients, particularly nitrogen. Also, adding fresh organic matter, such as garden debris, might encourage or introduce pests and diseases in your garden.

A compost pile or bin, which can be either built or purchased already assembled, creates a controlled environment where organic matter can be fully broken down before being added to your garden.

Creating compost is a simple process. Kitchen scraps, grass clippings and fall leaves will slowly break down if left in a pile. The process can be sped up by following a few simple guidelines.

Your compost pile should contain both dry and fresh materials, with a larger proportion of dry matter such as chopped straw, shredded leaves or sawdust. Fresh green matter, such as vegetable scraps, grass clippings or pulled weeds, breaks down quickly and produces nitrogen, which feeds the decomposer organisms while they break down the tougher dry matter.

Layer the green matter with the dry matter and mix in small amounts of garden soil or previously finished compost. The addition of soil or compost will introduce beneficial microorganisms. If the pile seems very dry, sprinkle some water between the layers—the compost should be moist but not soaking wet, like a wrung-out sponge. Adding nitrogen, like that found in fertilizer, will speed up decomposition. Avoid strong concentrations that can kill beneficial organisms.

Each week or two, use a pitchfork to turn the pile over or poke holes into it. This will help aerate the material, which will speed up decomposition. A compost pile that is kept aerated can generate a lot of heat. Temperatures can reach 160° F. or more. Such high temperatures destroy weed seeds and kill many damaging organisms. Most beneficial organisms are not killed until the temperature rises higher than 160° F. To monitor the temperature of the compost near the middle of the pile you will need a thermometer that is attached to a long probe, similar to a large meat thermometer. Turn your compost when the temperature reaches 160° F. Aerating the pile will stimulate the process to heat up again but prevent the temperatures from becoming high enough to kill the beneficial organisms.

Avoid adding any diseased or pest-ridden materials to your compost pile. If the damaging organisms are not destroyed they could be spread throughout your garden. If you do add material you suspect of harboring pests or diseases, add it near the center of the pile where the temperature is highest.

When you can no longer recognize the matter that you put into the compost bin, and the temperature no longer rises upon turning, your compost is ready to be mixed into your garden beds. Getting to this point can take as little as one month and will leave you with organic material that is rich in nutrients and beneficial organisms.

Compost can also be purchased from most garden centers.

# SELECTING ANNUALS

Many gardeners consider the trip to the local garden center to pick out their annual plants an important rite of spring. Other gardeners find it rewarding to start their own annuals from seed. There are benefits to both methods, and many gardeners choose to use a combination of the two. Purchasing annuals provides you with plants that are well grown and often already in bloom, which is useful if you don't have the room or the facilities to start seeds. Some seeds require specific conditions that are difficult to achieve in a house or they have erratic germination rates, which makes starting them yourself impractical. On the other hand, starting from seed may offer you a greater selection of species and varieties, because seed catalogs often list many more plants than are offered at garden centers. Starting annuals from seed is discussed on p. 29.

Purchased annual plants are grown in a variety of containers. Some are sold in individual pots, some in divided cell-packs and others in undivided trays. Each type has advantages and disadvantages.

Annuals in individual pots are usually well established and have plenty of space for root growth. These annuals have probably been seeded in flat trays and then transplanted into individual pots once they developed a few leaves. The cost of labor, pots and soil can make this option more expensive. If you are planting a large area you may also find it difficult to transport large numbers of plants.

Annuals in cell-packs are often inexpensive and hold several plants, making them easy to transport. These annuals suffer less root damage when transplanted than do annuals in undivided trays, but because each cell is quite small, plants may become rootbound quickly.

Annuals in undivided trays have plenty of room for root growth and can be left in the trays longer than in other types of containers. Their roots,

Painted-tongue

Root-bound seedling on left,
nicely rooted plant on right

Globe amaranth

however, tend to become entangled, making the plants difficult to separate.

Regardless of the type of container, the best plants to choose are often not yet flowering. These plants are younger and are less likely to be root-bound. Check for roots emerging from the holes at the bottom of the cells, or gently remove the plant from the container to look at the roots. Too many roots means that the plant is too mature for the container, especially if the roots are wrapped around the inside of the container in a thick web. Such plants are slow to establish once they are transplanted into the garden.

The plants should be compact and have good color. Healthy leaves look firm and vibrant. Unhealthy leaves may be wilted, chewed or discolored. Tall, leggy plants have likely been deprived of light. Sickly plants may not survive being transplanted and may spread pests or diseases to the rest of your garden.

Once you get your annuals home, water them if they are dry. Annuals growing in small containers may require water more than once a day. Begin to harden off the plants so they can be transplanted into the garden as soon as possible. Your annuals are probably accustomed to growing in the sheltered environment of a green-house, and they will need to become accustomed to the climate outdoors. They can be placed outdoors in a lightly shaded spot each day and brought into a sheltered porch, garage or house each night for about a week. This process will acclimatize them to your garden.

# Planting Annuals

Once your annuals are hardened off, it is time to plant them out. If your beds are already prepared you are ready to start. The only tool you are likely to need is a trowel. Be sure you have set aside enough time to do the job. You don't want to have young plants out of their pots and not finish planting them. If they are left out in the sun they can quickly dry out and die. To help avoid this problem choose an overcast day for planting.

If you have not prepared a flower bed by adding organic matter (see the section on Preparing the Garden, p. 23), add a trowelful of compost to the planting hole and mix it into the garden soil before adding your annual.

Moisten the soil to aid the removal of the plants from their containers. Push on the bottom of the cell or pot with your thumb to ease the plants out. If the plants were growing in an undivided tray then you will have to gently untangle the roots. If the roots are very tangled, immerse them in water and wash some of the soil away to help free the plants from one another. If you must handle the plant, hold it by a leaf to avoid crushing the stems. Remove and discard any damaged leaves or growth.

The rootball should contain a network of white plant roots. If the rootball is densely matted and twisted, break it apart in order to encourage the roots to extend and grow outward.

Informal planting

Three-tiered border

Do so by breaking apart the tangles a bit with your thumbs. New root growth will start from the breaks, allowing the plant to spread outwards.

Insert your trowel into the soil and pull it towards you, creating a wedge. Place your annual into the hole and firm the soil around the plant with your hands. Water newly planted annuals gently but thoroughly. Until they are established they will need regular watering for a few weeks.

You don't have to be conservative when arranging your flowerbeds. Though formal bedding-out patterns are still used in many parks and gardens, plantings can be made in casual groups and natural drifts. The quickest way to space out your annuals is to remove them from their containers and randomly place them on the bed. You can then mix colors and plants without too much planning. Plant a small section at a time—don't allow the roots to dry out. This is especially important if you have a large bed to plant.

If you are adding just a few annuals here and there to accent your shrub and perennial plantings, plant in groups. Random clusters of three to five plants add color and interest.

Combine low-growing or spreading annuals with tall or bushy ones. Keep the tallest plants towards the back and smallest plants towards the front of the bed. Doing so improves the visibility of the plants and hides the often unattractive lower limbs of taller plants. Be sure to leave your plants enough room to spread. They may look lonely and far apart when you first plant them, but annuals will quickly grow to fill in the space.

# ANNUALS FROM SEED

Starting annuals from seed can be fun and can provide you with a wider variety of annuals than that available as bedding plants. Dozens of catalogs from different growers offer a diverse selection of annuals that can be started from seed. Many gardeners while away chilly winter evenings by poring over seed catalogs and planning their spring and summer gardens.

Starting your own annuals can save you money, particularly if you need a lot of plants. The basic equipment necessary is not expensive, and most seeds can be started in a sunny window. However, you may encounter the problem of limited space. One or two trays of annuals don't take up too much room, but starting more than that may be unreasonable. For this reason, many gardeners start a few specialty plants themselves but purchase the bulk of their annuals as plants from a garden center.

Each plant in this book will have specific information on starting it from seed, but a few basic steps can be followed for all seeds. The easiest way for the home gardener to start seeds is to use cell-packs in trays with plastic

dome covers. The cell-packs keep roots separated, and the tray and dome keep moisture in.

Seeds can also be started in pots, peat pots or peat pellets. The advantage to starting in peat pots or pellets is that you will not disturb the roots when you transplant your annuals. When planting peat pots into the garden, be sure to remove the top couple of inches of pot. If any of the pot sticks up out of the soil, it can wick moisture away from the roots.

Use a growing mix (soil mix) intended for seedlings. These mixes are very fine, usually made from peat moss, vermiculite and perlite. The mix will have good water-holding capacity and will have been sterilized to prevent pests and diseases from attacking

Preparing seed trays

Using folded paper to plant small seeds

Watering seeds

Prepared seed tray

Sprouted seedlings with fluorescent light

your tender young seedlings. Fill your pots or seed trays with the soil mix and firm it down slightly. Soil that is too firmly packed will not drain well. Wet the soil before planting your seeds to prevent them from getting washed around. The easiest method is to wet the soil before you fill the trays or pots.

Large seeds can be planted one or two to a cell, but smaller seeds may have to be placed in a folded piece of paper and sprinkled evenly over the soil surface. Very tiny seeds, like those of begonia, can be mixed with fine sand before being sprinkled across the soil surface.

Small seeds will not need to be covered with any more soil, but medium-sized seeds can be lightly covered with soil, and large seeds can be poked into the soil. Some seeds need to be exposed to light in order to germinate; these should be left on the soil surface regardless of their size.

Place pots or flats of seeds in plastic bags to retain humidity while the seeds are germinating. Many planting trays come with clear plastic covers, which can be placed over the trays to keep the moisture in. Remove the plastic once the seeds have germinated.

Water seeds and small seedlings with a fine spray from a hand-held mister—small seeds can easily be washed around if the spray is too strong. I recall working at a greenhouse where the seed trays containing alyssum were once watered a little too vigorously. Alyssum was soon found growing just about everywhere—with other plants, in the gravel on the floor, even in some of the flowerbeds outside. The lesson is 'water gently.' A less hardy species would not have come up at all if its seeds were washed into an adverse location.

Seeds provide all the energy and nutrients that young seedlings require. Small seedlings will not need to be fertilized until they have about four or five true leaves. True leaves are the ones that look like the mature leaves. (The first one or two leaves are the cotyledons, or seed leaves.) When the first leaves that sprouted (the seed leaves) begin to shrivel, the plant has

Black-eyed Susan can be sown directly into the garden.

used up all its seed energy. You can then begin to use fertilizer diluted to one-quarter strength when feeding seedlings or young plants.

Take care to prevent **damping off,** a disease caused by soil-borne fungi. An afflicted seedling appears to have been pinched at soil level. The pinched area blackens and the seedling topples over and dies. Sterile soil mix, evenly moist soil and good air circulation will help prevent this problem.

If the seedlings get too big for their containers before you are ready to plant them out, you may have to pot them to prevent them from becoming root-bound. Harden plants off by exposing them to outdoor conditions for increasing periods of time every day for at least a week before planting them out.

To start seeds directly in the garden, begin with a well-prepared bed that has been smoothly raked. The small

Calendula (above)

Cleome (center), Love-in-a-mist (below)

furrows left by the rake will help hold moisture and prevent the seeds from being washed away. Sprinkle the seeds into the furrows and cover them lightly with peat moss or more soil. Larger seeds can be planted slightly deeper into the soil. You may not want to sow very tiny seeds directly in the garden because they can blow or wash away.

The soil should be kept moist to ensure even germination. Use a gentle spray to avoid washing the seeds around the bed or they will pool into dense clumps. Covering your newly seeded bed with chicken wire, an old sheet or some thorny branches will discourage animals from digging.

## ANNUALS FOR DIRECT SEEDING

Amaranth
Baby's Breath
Bachelor's Button
Black-eyed Susan
Calendula
California Poppy
Candytuft
Celosia
Cleome
Cosmos
Larkspur
Lavatera
Love-in-a-Mist
Nasturtium
Phlox
Poppy
Sunflower
Sweet Pea
Zinnia

# CARING FOR ANNUALS

Some annuals require more care than others do, but most require minimal care once established. Weeding, watering, fertilizing and deadheading are the basic tasks that, when performed regularly, will keep your garden looking its best. As well, some plants grown as annuals are actually perennials and may be overwintered with little effort.

## Weeding

Controlling weed populations keeps the garden healthy and neat. Weeding may not be anyone's favorite task, but it is essential. Weeds compete with your plants for light, nutrients and space, and they can harbor pests and diseases.

Weeds can be pulled by hand or with a hoe. Shortly after a rainfall, when the soil is soft and damp, is the easiest time to pull weeds. A hoe scuffed quickly across the soil surface will uproot small weeds and sever larger ones from their roots. Try to pull weeds out while they are still small. Once they are large enough to flower, many will quickly set seed; then you will have an entire new generation to worry about.

## Mulching

A layer of mulch around your plants will help keep weeds from germinating by preventing sufficient light from reaching the seeds. Those that do germinate will be smothered or will find it difficult to get to the soil surface, exhausting their energy before getting a chance to grow.

Mulch also helps maintain consistent soil temperatures and ensures that moisture is retained more effectively. In areas that receive heavy wind or rainfall, mulch can protect the soil and prevent erosion. Mulching is effective in both garden beds and planters.

Deadheading dahlias

Organic mulches include such materials as compost, bark chips, grass clippings or shredded leaves. These mulches add nutrients to soil as they break down, thus improving the quality of the soil and ultimately the health of your plants.

Spread about 2–3" of mulch over the soil after you have planted your annuals. Don't pile the mulch too thickly immediately around the crowns and stems of your annuals. Mulching right up against plants traps moisture and prevents air circulation, encouraging fungal disease.

As your mulch breaks down over summer, be sure to replenish it.

Mulched garden

## Watering

Water thoroughly but infrequently. Annuals given a light sprinkle of water every day will develop roots that stay close to the soil surface, making the plants vulnerable to heat and dry spells. Annuals given a deep watering once a week will develop a deeper root system. In a dry spell they will be adapted to seeking out the water trapped deeper in the ground.

Be sure the water penetrates at least 4" into the soil; this is equal to 1" of applied water. More water may be needed in very hot weather, when there is no rain. A mulch will slow water evaporation from the soil.

To save time, money and water you may wish to install an irrigation system. Irrigation systems apply the water exactly where it is needed, near the roots, and reduce the amount of water lost to evaporation. They can be very complex or very simple depending on your needs. A simple irrigation system would involve laying soaker hoses around your garden beds under the mulch. Consult with your local garden centers or landscape professionals for more information.

Annuals in hanging baskets and planters will need to be watered more frequently than plants in the ground. The smaller the container, the more often the plants will need watering. Containers and hanging moss baskets may need to be watered twice daily during hot, sunny weather.

## Fertilizing

Your local garden center should carry a good supply of both organic and chemical fertilizers. Always follow the directions carefully because using too

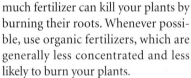

Hanging baskets

Ornamental yet functional sprinkler

much fertilizer can kill your plants by burning their roots. Whenever possible, use organic fertilizers, which are generally less concentrated and less likely to burn your plants.

Many annuals will flower most profusely if they are fertilized regularly. Some gardeners fertilize hanging baskets and container gardens every time they water, using a very dilute fertilizer so as not to burn the plants. Too much fertilizer can result in plants that produce weak growth that is susceptible to pest and disease problems. Some plants, such as nasturtiums, grow better without fertilizer and may produce few or no flowers when fertilized excessively.

Fertilizer comes in many forms. Liquids or water-soluble powders are easiest to use when watering. Slow-release pellets or granules are mixed into the garden or potting soil or sprinkled around the plant and left to work over summer.

## Grooming

Good grooming will keep your annuals looking neat, make them flower more profusely and help prevent pest and disease problems. Grooming may include pinching, deadheading, trimming and staking.

Pinch out (remove by hand or with scissors) any straggly growth and the tips of leggy annuals. Plants in cell-packs may have developed straggly growth trying to get light. Pinch back the long growth when planting to encourage bushier growth.

Some annuals have very tall growth and cannot be pinched. Remove the main shoot after it blooms to encourage side shoots to develop. Some tall annuals, such as larkspur, require staking with bamboo or other tall,

Spiral stakes

growth will sprout along with a second flush of flowers.

Deadheading, or removing faded flowers, is important in maintaining the health of annuals and in prolonging their bloom. Get into the habit of picking off spent flowers as you are looking around your garden; a little deadheading each day will save you a big job later. Some plants, such as impatiens and wax begonias, are self-cleaning, meaning that they drop their faded blossoms on their own and do not need deadheading.

## Growing Perennials as Annuals

Many plants grown as annuals are actually perennials, such as geranium, or shrubs, such as fuchsia, that originate in warmer climates and are unable to survive our cold winters. Other plants grown as annuals are biennials, such as Canterbury bells, and are started very early in the year to allow them to grow and flower in a single season. These perennials and biennials are listed as such in the individual entries in this book. You can use several techniques to keep these plants for more than one summer.

Some tropical perennials are given special treatment to help them survive winter, or they are simply brought inside and treated as houseplants in the colder months.

A reverse hardening-off process is used to acclimatize plants to an indoor environment. Plants such as geranium, black-eyed Susan vine and heliotrope, which are grown in the sun all summer, are gradually moved to shady garden spots. This gives them a chance to develop more efficient

thin stakes. Tie the plant loosely to the stake; strips of nylon hosiery make soft ties that won't cut into the plant. Stake bushy plants with twiggy branches or tomato cages. Insert the twigs or cages around the plant when it is small and it will grow to fill in and hide the stakes.

If annuals appear tired and withered by mid-summer, try trimming them back to encourage a second blooming. Mounding or low-growing annuals, such as petunias, respond well to trimming. Take your garden shears and trim back one-quarter to one-half of the plant growth. New

leaves, capable of surviving in the comparatively limited light indoors.

Perennials with tuberous roots can be stored over winter and replanted in late winter or early spring. Dig up plants such as dahlias, tuberous begonias and four o'clock flower in fall after the plant dies back but before the ground freezes. Shake the loose dirt away from the roots and let them dry out a bit in a cool dark place. Once they are dry, the rest of the soil should brush away. Dust the tubers with an anti-fungal powder (found at garden centers) before storing them in moist peat moss or coarse sawdust. Keep them in a dark, dry place that is cold but doesn't freeze. Pot them if they start to sprout, and keep them in a bright window and in moist soil. By late winter or early spring they should be potted up, whether they have already started sprouting or not, so they will be ready for spring planting.

Cuttings can be taken from large or fast-growing plants such as licorice plant, Mexican mint, geraniums and black-eyed Susan vine. Grow late-summer cuttings indoors in pots over winter for new spring plants.

If winter storage sounds like too much work, replace your annuals each year and leave the hard work to the growers.

Dahlia

Fuchsia

Canterbury bells

# Problems & Pests

New annuals are planted each spring, and often different species are grown each year. These factors make it difficult for pests and diseases to find their preferred host plants and establish a population. However, because annual species are often grown together in masses, any problems that do set in over summer are likely to attack all the plants.

For many years, pest control meant spraying or dusting, with the goal to eliminate every pest in the landscape. A more moderate approach advocated today is IPM (Integrated Pest Management or Integrated Plant Management). The goal of IPM is to reduce pest problems to levels at which only negligible damage is done. Of course, you must determine what degree of damage is acceptable to you. Consider whether a pest's damage is localized or covers the entire plant. Will the damage kill the plant or is it affecting only the outward appearance? Are there methods of controlling the pest without chemicals?

Chemicals should be used only as a last resort. They can endanger the gardener and his or her family and pets, and they kill good organisms along with bad, leaving the garden vulnerable to even worse attacks. A good IPM program includes learning about your plants and the conditions they need for healthy growth, what pests might affect your plants, where and when to look for those pests and how to control them. Keep records of pest damage because your observations can reveal patterns useful in spotting recurring problems and in planning your maintenance regime.

A responsible pest-management program has four steps. Cultural controls are the most important. Physical controls should be attempted next, followed by biological controls. Use chemical controls only when the other possibilities have been exhausted.

**Cultural controls** are the gardening techniques you use daily. Keeping your plants as healthy as possible is the best defense against pests. Growing annuals in the conditions they prefer and keeping your soil healthy, with plenty of organic matter, are just two of the cultural controls you can use to manage pests. Choose varieties of annuals that are resistant to problems. Space the plants so that they have good air circulation around them and are not stressed from competing for light, nutrients and space. Remove plants from the landscape if they are decimated by the same pests every year. Remove and burn or take to a permitted dump site diseased foliage and branches. Prevent the spread of disease by keeping your gardening tools clean and by tidying up fallen leaves and dead plant matter at the end of every growing season.

**Physical controls** are generally used to combat insect problems. An example of such a control is picking insects off plants by hand, which is not that daunting if you catch the problem when it is just beginning. Large, slow insects are particularly easy to pick off. Other physical controls include barriers that stop insects from getting to the plant, and traps that catch or confuse insects. Physical control of diseases often necessitates removing the infected part or parts of the plant to prevent the spread of the problem.

**Biological controls** make use of populations of natural predators. Such animals as birds, snakes, frogs, spiders, lady beetles and certain bacteria help keep pest populations at a manageable level. Encourage these creatures to take up permanent residence in your garden. A birdbath and birdfeeder will encourage birds to enjoy your yard and feed on a wide variety of insect pests. Many beneficial insects are probably already living in your landscape, and you can encourage them to stay by planting appropriate food sources. Many beneficial insects eat nectar from flowers such as the perennial yarrow.

Frogs eat many insect pests.

Chemical controls should rarely be necessary, but if you must use them there should be some 'organic' options available at garden centers. Organic sprays are no less dangerous than chemical ones, but they will break down into harmless compounds. The main drawback to using any chemicals is that they may also kill the beneficial insects you have been trying to attract to your garden. Follow the manufacturer's instructions carefully. A large amount of insecticide is not going to be any more effective in controlling pests than the recommended amount. Note that if a particular pest is not listed on the package, it will not be controlled by that product. Proper and early identification of pests is vital to finding a quick solution.

While cultural, physical, biological and chemical controls are all possible defenses against insects, diseases can be controlled only culturally. Weakened plants succumb to diseases more readily than healthy plants, although some diseases can infect plants regardless of their level of health. Prevention is often the only hope: once a plant has been infected, it should probably be destroyed in order to prevent the disease from spreading.

## Glossary of Pests & Diseases

### ANTHRACNOSE
Fungus. Yellow or brown spots on leaves; sunken lesions and blisters on stems; can kill plant.

**What to Do:** Choose resistant varieties and cultivars; keep soil well drained; thin out stems to improve air circulation; avoid handling wet foliage. Remove and destroy infected plant parts; clean up and destroy debris from infected plants at end of growing season.

### APHIDS
Tiny, pear-shaped insects, winged or wingless; green, black, brown, red or gray. Cluster along stems, on buds and on leaves. Suck sap from plants; cause distorted or stunted growth. Sticky honeydew forms on surfaces and encourages sooty mold growth.

**What to Do:** Squish small colonies by hand; dislodge them with water spray; many predatory insects and birds feed on them; spray serious infestations with insecticidal soap or neem oil.

### ASTER YELLOWS
Transmitted by leafhoppers. Acts like a virus, causing stunted or deformed growth, yellowed and deformed leaves, dwarfed and greenish flowers; can kill plant.

**What to Do:** Control leafhoppers with insecticidal soap; remove and destroy infected plants; destroy any local weeds sharing the symptoms. Disease cannot be cured.

### BEETLES
Many types and sizes; usually rounded in shape with hard, shell-like outer wings covering membranous inner wings. Some are beneficial, e.g., ladybird beetles ('ladybugs'); others, e.g., June beetles, eat plants. Larvae: see Borers, Grubs. Leave wide range of chewing damage: make small or large holes in or around margins of leaves; consume entire leaves or areas between leaf veins ('skeletonize'); may also chew holes in flowers.

**What to Do:** Pick beetles off at night and drop them into an old coffee can half filled with soapy water (soap prevents them from floating); spread an old sheet under plants and shake off beetles to collect and dispose of them. Spray heavy infestations with neem oil.

## BLIGHT

Fungal diseases, many types, e.g., leaf blight, gray mold (Botrytis blight), snow blight. Leaves, stems and flowers blacken, rot and die.

**What to Do:** Thin stems to improve air circulation; keep mulch away from base of plant; remove debris from garden at end of growing season. Remove and destroy infected plant parts.

## BORERS

Larvae of some moths, wasps, beetles; among the most damaging plant pests. Burrow into plant stems, branches, leaves and/or roots; destroy vascular tissue (plant veins and arteries) and structural strength. Worm-like; vary in size and get bigger as they bore through plants. Burrow and weaken stems to cause breakage; leaves will wilt; may see tunnels in leaves, stems or roots; rhizomes may be hollowed out entirely or in part.

**What to Do:** May be able to squish within leaves. Remove and destroy bored parts; may need to dig up and destroy infected roots and rhizomes.

## BUGS (TRUE BUGS)

Small insects, up to $1/2$" long; green, brown, black or brightly colored and patterned. Many beneficial; a few pierce plants to suck out sap. Toxins may be injected that deform plants; sunken areas left where pierced; leaves rip as they grow; leaves, buds and new growth may be dwarfed and deformed.

**What to Do:** Remove debris and weeds from around plants in fall to destroy overwintering sites. Pick off by hand and drop into soapy water; spray plants with insecticidal soap.

## CATERPILLARS

Larvae of butterflies, moths, sawflies. Include bagworms, budworms, case bearers, cutworms, leaf rollers, leaf tiers, loopers. Chew foliage and buds; can completely defoliate a plant if infestation severe.

**What to Do:** Removal from plant is best control. Use a strong spray of water and soap or pick caterpillars off by hand if plant is small enough. Control biologically using the naturally occuring soil bacterium *Bacillus thuringiensis* var. *kurstaki* or *B.t.* for short (commercially available), which breaks down gut lining of caterpillars. Can also use neem oil.

### DAMPING OFF
see p. 31

Ladybird beetle

Ladybird beetle larvae

## GALLS

Unusual swellings of plant tissues. Can affect leaves, buds, stems, flowers, fruit. May be caused by insects or diseases. Often a gall affects a single genus or species.

**What to Do:** Cut galls out of plant and destroy them. Galls caused by insects usually contain the insect's eggs and juvenile forms. Prevent these galls by controlling insect before it lays eggs; otherwise try to remove and destroy infected tissue before the young insects emerge. Generally insect galls are more unsightly than damaging to plants. Galls caused by diseases often require destruction of plant. Avoid placing other plants susceptible to same disease in that location.

## GRAY MOLD

see Blight

## GRUBS

Larvae of different beetles, commonly found below soil level; usually curled in C-shape. Body white or gray; head may be white, gray, brown or reddish. Problematic in lawns; may feed on plant roots. Plant wilts despite regular watering; may pull easily out of ground in severe cases.

**What to Do:** Toss any grubs found while digging onto a stone path or patio for birds to devour; apply parasitic nematodes or milky disease spore to infested soil (ask at your local garden center).

## LEAFHOPPERS

Small, wedge-shaped insects; can be green, brown, gray or multi-colored. Jump around frantically when disturbed. Suck juice from plant leaves. Cause distorted growth. Carry diseases such as aster yellows.

**What to Do:** Encourage predators by planting nectar-producing species like yarrow. Wash insects off with strong spray of water; spray with insecticidal soap or neem oil.

## LEAF MINERS

Tiny, stubby larvae of some butterflies and moths; may be yellow or green. Tunnel within leaves leaving winding trails; tunneled areas lighter in color than rest of leaf. Unsightly rather than health risk to plant.

**What to Do:** Remove debris from area in fall to destroy overwintering sites; attract parasitic wasps with nectar plants such as yarrow. Remove and destroy infected foliage; can sometimes squish by hand within leaf.

## LEAF SPOT

Two common types. *Bacterial:* small speckled spots grow to encompass entire leaves; brown or purple in color; leaves may drop. *Fungal:* black, brown or yellow spots; leaves wither.

**What to Do:** Bacterial infection more severe; must remove entire plant. For

Lygus bug

Caterpillar

fungal infection, remove and destroy infected plant parts. Sterilize removal tools; avoid wetting foliage or touching wet foliage; remove and destroy debris at end of growing season. Spray plant with neem oil for fungal infection.

### MEALYBUGS

Tiny crawling insects related to aphids; appear to be covered with white fuzz or flour. Sucking damage stunts and stresses plant. Mealybugs excrete honeydew that promotes growth of sooty mold.

**What to Do:** Remove by hand on smaller plants; wash plant off with soap and water; wipe off with alcohol-soaked swabs; remove leaves with heavy infestations; encourage or introduce natural predators such as mealybug destroyer beetle and parasitic wasps; spray with insecticidal soap or neem oil. Keep in mind larvae of mealybug destroyer beetles look like very large mealybugs.

### MILDEW

Two types, both caused by fungus, but with slightly different symptoms. *Downy mildew:* yellow spots on upper sides of leaves and downy fuzz on undersides; fuzz may be yellow, white or gray. *Powdery mildew:* white or gray powdery coating on leaf surfaces, doesn't brush off.

**What to Do:** Choose resistant cultivars; space plants well; thin stems to encourage air circulation; tidy any debris in fall.

Remove and destroy infected leaves or other parts. Spray with neem oil.

### MITES

Tiny, eight-legged relatives of spiders. Almost invisible to naked eye; red, yellow or green; usually found on undersides of plant leaves. May see fine webbing on leaves and stems; may see mites moving on leaf undersides; leaves become discolored and speckled, then turn brown and shrivel up.

**What to Do:** Wash off with strong spray of water daily until all signs of infestation are gone; predatory mites available through garden centers; spray plants with insecticidal soap or neem oil.

### MOSAIC

see Viruses

### NEMATODES

Tiny worms that give plants disease symptoms. One type infects foliage and stems; the other infects roots. *Foliar:* yellow spots that turn brown on leaves; leaves shrivel and wither; problem starts on lowest leaves and works up plant. *Root-knot:* plant is stunted; may wilt; yellow spots on leaves; roots have tiny bumps or knots.

**What to Do:** Mulch soil, add organic matter, clean up debris in fall. Don't touch wet foliage of infected plants; can add parasitic nematodes to soil. Remove infected plants in extreme cases.

Leaf miner damage

Powdery mildew

## ROT

Several different fungi that affect different parts of the plant and can kill plant. *Crown rot (stem rot):* affects base of plant, causing stems to blacken and fall over and leaves to yellow and wilt. *Root rot:* leaves yellow and plant wilts; digging up plant will show roots rotted away.

**What to Do:** Keep soil well drained; don't damage plant if you are digging around it; keep mulches away from plant base. Destroy infected plant if whole plant affected.

## RUST

Fungi. Pale spots on upper leaf surfaces; orange, fuzzy or dusty spots on leaf undersides.

**What to Do:** Choose rust-resistant varieties and cultivars; avoid handling wet leaves; provide plant with good air circulation; clear up garden debris at end of season. Remove and destroy infected plant parts. Spray with neem oil.

## SCALE INSECTS

Tiny, shelled insects that suck sap, weakening and possibly killing plant or making it vulnerable to other problems. Once female scale insect has pierced plant with mouthpart, it is there for life. Juvenile scale insects are called crawlers.

**What to Do:** Wipe off with alcohol-soaked swabs; spray with water to dislodge crawlers; encourage natural predators and parasites; dispose of infected material carefully at end of summer.

## SLUGS & SNAILS

Both mollusks; slugs lack shells, snails have spiral shells. Up to 8" long, many smaller. Slimy, smooth skin; gray, green, black, beige, yellow or spotted. Leave large, ragged holes in leaves and silvery slime trails on and around plants.

**What to Do:** Attach strips of copper to wood around raised beds or to smaller boards inserted around susceptible groups of plants; slugs and snails get shocked if they touch copper surfaces. Pick off by hand in the evening and squish with boot or drop in can of soapy water. Spread wood ash or diatomaceous earth (available in garden centers) on ground around plants; it will pierce their soft bodies and cause them to dehydrate. Do not use diatomaceous earth intended for swimming pool filters. Slug baits containing iron phosphate are not harmful to humans or animals and control slugs very well when used according to package directions. If slugs damaged garden last season, begin controls as soon as new green shoots appear in spring.

## SMUT

Fungus. May cause galls or streaking on leaves.

**What to Do:** Treat as for rust.

Snail

Slug

## SOOTY MOLD

Fungus. Thin black film forms on leaf surfaces and reduces amount of light getting to leaves.

**What to Do:** Wipe mold off leaf surfaces; control insects such as aphids, mealybugs, whiteflies (honeydew left on leaves encourages mold).

## THRIPS

Difficult to see; may be visible if you disturb them by blowing gently on an infested flower. Yellow, black or brown; tiny, slender, with narrow fringed wings. Suck juice out of plant cells, particularly in flowers and buds, causing mottled petals and leaves, dying buds and distorted and stunted growth.

**What to Do:** Remove and destroy infected plant parts; encourage native predatory insects with nectar plants like yarrow; spray severe infestations with insecticidal soap or neem oil.

## VIRUSES

Plant may be stunted and leaves and flowers distorted, streaked or discolored. Example: tobacco mosaic virus.

**What to Do:** Viral diseases in plants cannot be controlled.Destroy infected plants; disinfect tools that have been used on virus-infected plants; control insects like aphids, leafhoppers and whiteflies that spread disease.

## WHITEFLIES

Flying insects that flutter up into the air when the plant is disturbed. Tiny; moth-like; white; live on undersides of plant leaves. Suck juice out of plant leaves, causing yellowed leaves and weakened plants; leave sticky honeydew on leaves, encouraging sooty mold growth.

**What to Do:** Destroy weeds where insects may live. Attract native predatory beetles and parasitic wasps with nectar plants like yarrow; spray severe cases with insecticidal soap. Can make a sticky flypaper-like trap by mounting tin can on stake; wrap can with yellow paper and cover with clear plastic bag smeared with petroleum jelly; replace bag when full of flies.

## WILT

If watering hasn't helped a wilted plant, one of two wilt fungi may be at fault. *Fusarium wilt:* plant wilts, leaves turn yellow then die; symptoms generally appear first on one part of plant before spreading to other parts. *Verticillium wilt:* plant wilts; leaves curl up at edges; leaves turn yellow then drop off; plant may die.

**What to Do:** Both wilts are difficult to control. Choose resistant plant varieties and cultivars; clean up debris at end of growing season. Destroy infected plants; solarize (sterilize) soil before replanting (this may help if you've lost an entire bed of plants to these fungi)—contact local garden center for assistance.

## WORMS

see Caterpillars, Nematodes

---

### Insecticidal soap recipe

*You can make your own insecticidal soap. Mix 1 tsp. of mild dish detergent or pure soap (biodegradable options are available) with 1 qt. of water in a clean spray bottle. Spray the surfaces of your plants and rinse well within an hour of spraying to avoid foliage discoloration.*

---

Mosaic virus

# ABOUT THIS GUIDE

The annuals in this book are organized alphabetically by their most familiar, local common names. Other common names and scientific names appear after the primary reference, and all names can be found in the index. The illustrated **Flowers at a Glance** section at the beginning of the book will familiarize you with the different flowers quickly, and it will help you find a plant if you aren't sure what it's called.

Clearly indicated at the beginning of each entry are height and spread ranges and flower colors. At the back of the book, you will find a **Quick Reference Chart** that summarizes different features and requirements of the annuals; you will find this chart handy when planning diversity in your garden.

Each entry gives clear instructions and tips for seeding, planting and growing the annual, and it recommends many of our favorite species and varieties. *Note:* If height and spread ranges are not indicated for a recommended plant, assume these values are the same as the ranges at the beginning of the entry. Keep in mind, too, that many more hybrids, cultivars and varieties are often available. Check with your local greenhouses or garden centers when making your selection.

Pests or diseases that commonly afflict a plant, if any, are also listed for each entry. Consult the 'Problems & Pests' section of the introduction for information on how to solve these problems.

# The
# Annuals

# Abutilon
## Flowering Maple, Chinese Lantern
*Abutilon*

**Height:** 18–36" **Spread:** 18–24" **Flower color:** red, pink, white, orange, yellow

ONE OF MY FIRST HOUSEPLANTS WAS A VARIEGATED ABUTILON, also known as flowering maple. Imagine—a maple growing in my college apartment! I was surprised to learn later that this plant is actually related to hollyhocks, and not to maples at all. It is a tender perennial that was popular in Victorian parlors and gardens. Its deeply cupped flowers come in vivid reds, pinks and oranges as well as subtle lemons and peaches. The incised, maple-like leaves vary in color from deep green to stippled greens and yellows. Abutilon is susceptible to whiteflies and mealybugs. If your non-variegated abutilon suddenly develops a stippled or mottled appearance, check for unwanted guests.

*This plant is in the mallow family and is not related to maples, as one of the common names suggests.*

## Planting

**Seeding:** Indoors in early winter with soil at 70°–75° F; blooms in 5–6 months from seed

**Planting out:** After last frost

**Spacing:** 24"

## Growing

Abutilon grows well in **full sun** but can benefit from some shade during the afternoon. The soil should be **average to fertile, moist** and **well drained.** Pinch back growing tips to encourage bushy growth.

## Tips

Include abutilon in borders and mixed containers. Container-grown plants are easier to bring indoors, where they will continue to bloom for most of the fall and winter. Indoor plants will need a bright window and should be allowed to dry out between waterings in winter.

## Recommended

*A.* x *hybridum (A. globosum)* is a bushy, mound-forming shrub that can be treated as an annual or wintered indoors and moved outside for the summer. Drooping, cup- or trumpet-shaped flowers are borne for most of the summer. Named varieties are available, but most seed catalogs sell seeds in mixed packets, so flower colors will be a surprise.

## Problems & Pests

Few problems occur in the garden, but whiteflies, mealybugs and scale insects can cause trouble when plants are moved indoors.

*Abutilon is one of the few plants that, depending on the climate, may be grown as an annual, a perennial or a shrub.*

# African Daisy
## Monarch of the Veldt
*Arctotis (Venidium)*

**Height:** 12–24"  **Spread:** 12–16"  **Flower color:** pink, orange, yellow, red, white

SOUTH AFRICA HAS GIVEN US A PROFUSION OF ANNUAL DAISIES. It is often difficult to tell one from the other, and the difference is usually in how they perform in your garden. African daisies are intensely colored, and I find that I choose these beauties not by their cultivar names, but by which color resonates with my buying mood. Because African daisies fully open only in the sun, it is important to place them correctly. If you like looking at the undersides of the petals, use blue-eyed African daisy—its petal undersides are a delicate lavender.

*African daisies make interesting cut flowers, but they close up at night and in rooms that are not very bright.*

## Planting

**Seeding:** Indoors in early spring; direct sow after last frost

**Planting out:** Once soil has warmed

**Spacing:** 12–16"

## Growing

Choose a location in **full sun**. The soil should be **average, moist** and **well drained**. African daisies don't mind sandy soil, and they tolerate drought well. Keep the plants deadheaded and they will flower continuously from mid-summer to frost.

Seeds started indoors should be planted in peat pots or peat pellets to avoid disturbing the roots when transplanting. African daisy seeds do not keep long, so purchase or collect new seeds each year.

## Tips

African daisies can be grouped or massed in beds, borders and cutting gardens. They do quite well when grown in planters and other containers. You can try growing a fall crop—sow seeds directly in the garden in mid-summer and enjoy the flowers all fall.

## Recommended

*A. fastuosa* (monarch of the veldt, Cape daisy) has bright orange flowers with a purple spot at the base of each petal. It grows 12–24" tall and spreads 12". **'Zulu Prince'** bears large cream white or yellow flowers with bands of brown and orange at the base of each petal. The deeply lobed leaves are silvery white.

*A.* x *hybrida* (Harlequin Hybrids) grow up to 20" tall and spread 12".

*A.* x *hybrida* (photos this page)

They do not come true from seed and are propagated by cuttings. The striking flowers may be pink, red, white, orange or yellow.

*A. stoechadifolia* var. *grandis* (blue-eyed African daisy) has 3" wide, white blooms with a yellow ring, and the undersides of the petals are pale lavender blue. The plant has a nice bushy form and grows 24" tall and 16" wide.

## Problems & Pests

Watch for aphids, leaf miners, downy mildew and leaf spot.

# Ageratum
## Floss Flower
*Ageratum*

**Height:** 6–36" **Spread:** 6–18" **Flower color:** white, pink, mauve, blue

AGERATUM USED TO BE ON MY LIST OF ANNUALS TO AVOID. IT WAS planted everywhere. Then I realized that it is an amazing butterfly magnet. Ageratum offers a constant supply of nectar to many butterfly species throughout the summer and fall. Consider planting the taller 'Blue Horizon' in the middle of the bed with *Verbena bonariensis* in the back and the zinnia cultivars 'Crystal White' and 'Profusion Orange' up front. All four attract butterflies and other pollinators, providing constant entertainment.

## Planting

**Seeding:** Indoors in early spring; direct sow after last frost. Don't cover the seeds; they need light to germinate.

**Planting out:** Once soil has warmed

**Spacing:** 4–12"

## Growing

Ageratum prefers **full sun** but tolerates partial shade. The soil should be **fertile, moist** and **well drained**. This plant doesn't like to have its soil dry out; a moisture-retaining mulch will reduce the necessary watering frequency. Don't mulch too thickly or too close to the base of the plant or it may develop crown rot or root rot.

Though this plant needs deadheading to keep it flowering, the blossoms are extraordinarily long-lived, making ageratum an easy-care plant for sunny gardens.

'Blue Hawaii'

*The genus* Ageratum *comprises about 40 species of annuals, perennials and shrubs. Naturalized in many warm areas, they range from tropical South America to warm-temperate North America.*

'Blue Horizon' (above), *A. houstonianum* (below)

## Tips

The smaller varieties, which become almost completely covered with the fluffy flowerheads, make excellent edging plants for flowerbeds. They are also attractive grouped in masses or grown in planters. The taller varieties are useful in the center of a flowerbed and make interesting cut flowers.

The original species is a tall, leggy plant that was not considered attractive enough for the annual border but was used in the cutting garden. New cultivars are much more compact, and ageratum is now a proudly displayed annual.

## Recommended

*A. houstonianum* forms a large, leggy mound that can grow up to 24" tall. Clusters of fuzzy blue, white or pink flowers are held above the foliage. Many cultivars are available; most have been developed to maintain a low, compact form that is more useful in the border. **'Bavaria'** grows about 10" tall with blue-and-white bicolored flowers. **'Blue Hawaii'** is a compact plant 6–8" tall, with blue flowers. **'Blue Horizon'** is an upright cultivar with lavender blue flowers. It grows 24–36" tall. **'Pinky Improved'** is a compact plant with subtle, dusky pink flowers. **'Summer Snow'** has white flowers.

*The genus name* Ageratum *is derived from a Greek word meaning 'without age,' a reference to the long-lasting flowers.*

## Problems & Pests

Powdery mildew may become a problem. Be sure to plant ageratum in a location with good air circulation to help prevent fungal diseases.

*To dry ageratum flowers for crafts and floral arrangements, cut fresh flowers in the morning, bundle them together with rubber bands and hang them upside down in a location with good air circulation.*

'Blue Hawaii'

# Alyssum
## Sweet Alyssum
### *Lobularia*

**Height:** 3–12" **Spread:** 6–24" **Flower color:** pink, purple, yellow, salmon, white

ALYSSUM IS EXCELLENT FOR CREATING SOFT EDGES, AND MOST OF its colors blend well with other plants. 'New Lemon' adds a subtle yellow shimmer that is enhanced by cool weather, while 'Snow Crystal' sparkles in the sun. Alyssum can also scent a large area. I have it planted along the walk to my front door, where its light, flowery scent gives an olfactory welcome to visitors. But there is another side to the scent. Take a few long, deep breaths and see if your nose is sensitive enough to detect the underlying notes of overcooked cabbage. Here you have a clue to the plant's genealogy—like cabbage, it belongs to the mustard family.

## Planting

**Seeding:** Indoors in late winter, or direct sow in spring; often self-seeds

**Planting out:** Once soil has warmed

**Spacing:** 8–12"

## Growing

Alyssum prefers **full sun** but tolerates light shade. **Well-drained** soil with **average fertility** is preferred, but poor soil is tolerated. This plant dislikes having its roots disturbed, so if starting it indoors, use peat pots or pellets. Alyssum may die back a bit during the heat and humidity of our Ohio summers. Trim it back and water it periodically to encourage new growth and more flowers when the weather cools.

'Pastel Carpet'

Leave alyssum plants out all winter. In spring, remove the previous year's growth to expose self-sown seedlings below.

## Tips

Alyssum will creep around rock gardens, over rock walls and along the edges of beds. It is an excellent choice for seeding into cracks and crevices of walkway and patio stones, and once established it readily reseeds. It is also good for filling in spaces between taller plants in borders and mixed containers.

## Recommended

*L. maritima* forms a low, spreading mound of foliage. The entire plant appears to be covered in tiny blossoms when in full flower. '**New Lemon**' has cream flowers with a hint of yellow, most noticeable in cooler weather. '**Pastel Carpet**' bears flowers in rose, white, violet and mauve. '**Snow Crystal**' ('Snow Crystals') bears large, bright white flowers profusely all summer. **Wonderland Series** offers a mix of colors on compact plants.

## Problems & Pests

Alyssum rarely has problems but is sometimes afflicted with downy mildew.

Alyssum, *the original genus name for this annual, comes from the Greek and means 'not madness,' referring to the belief that the plant could cure rabies.*

# Amaranth

## *Amaranthus*

**Height:** 3–5' **Spread:** 12–30" **Flower color:** red, yellow, green; flowers inconspicuous in some species grown for foliage

THE SPECIES OF AMARANTH THAT ARE USED in the garden appear to be so different. Love-lies-bleeding *(A. caudatus)* forms bold, weeping stems of furry-looking flowers. Make sure you have something wonderful planted underneath because observers' eyes are sure to travel down to where the flower stems are pointing. In contrast, Joseph's coat *(A. tricolor)* boasts gorgeous leaves of many colors. A mass of Joseph's coat is a visual feast of golds, scarlets and burgundies. The amaranths are bold accents in the garden and blend in well with the current tropical-look garden style.

*Several species of* Amaranthus *are used as potherbs and vegetables because the leaves are high in protein; other species are grown as cereal crops.*

## Planting

**Seeding:** Indoors about three weeks before last frost; direct sow once soil has warmed

**Planting out:** Once soil has warmed

**Spacing:** 12–24"

## Growing

A location in **full sun** is preferable. The soil should be **poor to average** and **well drained.** Don't give these plants rich soil or overfertilize them, or their growth will be tall, soft and prone to falling over. Joseph's coat will also lose some of its leaf color if overfertilized; its colors will be more brilliant in poor soil.

Seeds started indoors should be planted in peat pots or pellets to avoid disturbing the roots when transplanting them.

Love-lies-bleeding self-seeds and can show up year after year. Unwanted plants are easy to uproot when they are young.

*A. caudatus* (above), *A. caudatus* cultivar (below)

'Viridis'

## Tips

Love-lies-bleeding is attractive grouped in borders or in mixed containers, where it requires very little care or water. Joseph's coat is a bright, striking plant that is best used as an annual specimen plant in a small group rather than in a large mass planting, where it quickly becomes overwhelming. It is also attractive mixed with large foliage plants in the back of a border.

## Recommended

*A. caudatus* (love-lies-bleeding, tassel flower, velvet flower) has long, drooping, rope-like, fluffy red, yellow or green flower spikes that can be air dried. The plant has erect stems and grows 3–5' tall and 18–30" wide. **'Love Lies Bleeding'** bears dark red tassels of flowers. **'Viridis'** bears tassels of light green flowers.

'Love Lies Bleeding'

*Amaranth has astringent properties and has been used by herbalists to stop bleeding and to treat diarrhea.*

*A. tricolor* (Joseph's coat) is a bushy, upright plant that grows up to 5' tall and 12–24" in spread. The brightly colored foliage is variegated and can be green, red, bronze, chocolaty purple, orange, yellow or gold. The flowers of the species and its cultivars are inconspicuous. The cultivar **'Illumination'** has hanging foliage in crimson and gold. It grows 4' tall and 12" wide. **'Joseph's Coat'** has green, yellow and bronze lower leaves and red and gold new leaves.

## Problems & Pests

Cold nights below 50° F will cause leaf drop. Rust, leaf spot, root rot, aphids and some viral diseases are potential problems.

'Joseph's Coat' (below), 'Illumination' (above)

*In ancient Greece, amaranth was regarded as a symbol of fidelity and immortality. The flowers were used to decorate tombs.*

# Anagallis
## Pimpernel
*Anagallis*

**Height:** 6–18"  **Spread:** 8–18"  **Flower color:** red, white, blue, pink

I WAS INTRODUCED TO ANAGALLIS BY *THE SCARLET PIMPERNEL*, a novel by Baroness Orczy. Curious, I looked up this European plant and found that it is considered a rather invasive but attractive little weed. The flower color is very interesting, scarlet with a bluish cast. Conversely, the blue pimpernel has blue flowers with a red to scarlet cast. As their colors are opposite, so are their weather preferences. Ohio gardeners tend to be more successful with blue pimpernel, which tolerates warm weather. During our hot, humid summers, scarlet pimpernel will stall, but maybe this tendency is fortunate; it might otherwise take over the garden.

*Anagallis species are in the same family as primroses.*

## Planting

**Seeding:** Start indoors in late winter

**Planting out:** Around last frost date

**Spacing:** 12–18"

## Growing

Anagallis prefer **full sun**. The soil should be **fertile, moist** and **well drained**. These plants do not tolerate compacted or clay soils.

## Tips

These low-growing plants make a colorful addition to the front of a border. They are useful in a new rock garden where slower-growing alpine plants have not yet filled in.

Be careful when handling these plants; touching the leaves may cause a skin rash.

## Recommended

*A. arvensis* (scarlet pimpernel) is a low, trailing plant that grows up to 6" tall and spreads up to 18". It bears red or white flowers that close on cloudy days and at night. This species prefers cool weather and may stop flowering in summer.

*A. monellii* (blue pimpernel) is low growing but more upright than *A. arvensis*. It grows 8–18" tall, with an equal spread, and bears blue, white, pink or red flowers. This species prefers warm weather. **'Skylover'** is an upright plant from Proven Winners. It bears deep blue flowers, larger than the flowers of the species.

## Problems & Pests

Aphids can be a problem.

'Skylover' (photos this page)

*Because its blooms close in the late afternoon and before a rain, scarlet pimpernel has also been called 'shepherd's clock' and 'poor man's weather glass.'*

# Angel's Trumpet
## Datura, Trumpet Flower, Jimsonweed
### *Brugmansia, Datura*

---

**Height:** 3–10' **Spread:** 3–6' **Flower color:** white, yellow, purple, pink

ALL ANGEL'S TRUMPETS ADD AN EXOTIC ACCENT TO THE GARDEN with their elegant, funnel-shaped flowers. Many are strongly fragrant—and they can almost literally take your breath away. Standing next to a large potted *Brugmansia* in full, glorious bloom, I noticed I was becoming a bit lightheaded. Moving away fixed the problem. Many *Datura* species are weeds across much of the U.S. One common name, locoweed, refers to the fact that after they eat the flowers, cattle act crazy. All parts of angel's trumpet plants contain toxins. The potency varies, and ingestion can be a fatal experience.

### Planting

**Seeding:** Slow to germinate. Start indoors in mid-winter; may not grow to flowering size until late summer. *Datura* will self-sow.

**Planting out:** Once soil has warmed and frost danger has passed

**Spacing:** 24–36"

*Jimsonweed (most often referring to D. stramonium) takes its name from Jamestown, Virginia, where soldiers sent to quell the rebellion in 1676 were poisoned by eating this plant.*

## Growing

Angel's trumpets prefer **full sun**. The soil should be **fertile, moist** and **well drained**. Water sparingly, just enough to keep the soil from drying out. Don't allow plants to completely dry out, particularly during hot, dry weather. Plants recover quickly from wilting when watered.

Propagate seeds indoors in early or mid-winter. Have patience because the seeds can be slow to germinate. Keep the soil moist but not soggy. These plants have become more popular in recent years, and many garden centers carry started plants.

## Tips

Angel's trumpet flowers tend to open at night. Grow these plants where you will be able to enjoy their intoxicating scent in the evening—near a patio or in a large container on a deck. If angel's trumpets are planted under an open window, the scent will carry into the room. These plants are attractive as specimens or in groups.

## Recommended

These plants have been divided into two different, but closely related, genera: *Datura* and *Brugmansia*. In general, herbaceous annuals and perennials with upward-facing flowers are classified as *Datura* while the woody plants with pendulous flowers are classified as *Brugmansia*. This rule of thumb is only slightly helpful because many of the woody plants are treated as tender annuals or perennials and are discarded before they become woody. As well, many

'Charles Grimaldi' (above), *B.* x *candida* (below)

'Cornucopia' (above), *D. metel* (below)

catalogs and garden centers name the plants incorrectly, and even the scientific names of the various species are in a state of confusion. So, find the plant you like and try not to worry too much about its name.

*B. aurea (D. aurea)* is a woody plant that can be grown indoors in a cool, bright room in winter and outdoors in summer. When grown outdoors, it bears bright yellow or white, scented flowers all summer. In the tropics this plant may grow as tall as 30', but in a container or border it will rarely grow taller than 5'. Growth can be easily controlled by trimming.

*B. x candida (B. aurea x B. versicolor)* is a woody plant that can be grown in a bright room indoors in winter and moved outdoors in summer. In a container it rarely grows over 10'. Trim it back to keep the size you want. It bears fragrant, white, trumpet-shaped flowers that may open only at night. **'Grand Marnier'** has apricot yellow flowers. The hybrids in the **Queen Series** are commonly available, often offered in seed catalogs. **'Golden Queen'** has yellow double flowers. **'Purple Queen'** also has double flowers; the inner petals are white and the outer petals are purple.

*B.* **'Charles Grimaldi'** is another woody plant. The large, funnel-shaped, pendulous flowers are lemon yellow. This is an excellent container plant for a patio or deck. In a container it rarely grows over 10'.

***D. innoxia*** (*D. meteloides;* downy thorn apple) is a small tender perennial grown as an annual. It grows 3' tall and, if allowed, can sprawl to 5–6'. The flowers are white, pink or lavender.

***D. metel*** (horn of plenty, jimsonweed, locoweed) is an annual that easily self-seeds. It grows to 3–4' tall and wide. The species produces single flowers, but many double- and even triple-flowered cultivars are available. **'Cornucopia'** has double purple and white flowers.

'Cornucopia' (above), *B. aurea* (below)

## Problems & Pests

Problems with whiteflies, spider mites and mealybugs are possible, though more likely on plants grown indoors.

*Angel's trumpets are in the potato family, the same family as the deadly nightshades. All parts of these plants are poisonous. Eating less than $1/2$ oz. of angel's trumpet seeds can be fatal.*

# Angelonia
## Angel Wings, Summer Snapdragon
*Angelonia*

**Height:** 12–24" **Spread:** 12" **Flower color:** purple, blue, white

BEING PARTIAL TO BLUE AND PURPLE IN THE garden, I was immediately attracted to angelonia when I first saw it in 2000. Angelonia is actually a tender subshrub native to Mexico and the West Indies. If you try to overwinter this plant, you will see that it forms a woody base and its growing habit changes to become more open and rangy. Most gardeners will probably find it preferable to either take cuttings or buy new plants each season. Seed is generally not available, and even if it were, angelonia probably would need to grow for two to three years before flowering.

### Planting
**Seeding:** Not recommended

**Planting out:** In warm soil after last frost

**Spacing:** 8–12"

*The individual flowers look a bit like orchid blossoms, but angelonia is actually in the same family as snapdragons.*

## Growing

Angelonia prefers **full sun** but tolerates a bit of shade. The soil should be **fertile, moist** and **well drained**. Though this plant grows naturally in damp areas, such as along ditches and near ponds, it is fairly drought tolerant.

Angel Mist Series (photos this page)

This tender subshrub is not worth trying to save from year to year because it tends to lose its attractive habit as it matures. Cuttings can be taken in late summer and grown indoors over the winter to be used the following summer.

## Tips

With its loose, airy spikes of orchid-like flowers, angelonia makes a welcome addition to the annual or mixed border. Include it in a pondside or streamside planting or in a mixed planter.

## Recommended

*A. angustifolia* is a perennial that is treated as an annual. It is a bushy, upright plant with loose spikes of flowers in varied shades of purple. 'Alba' bears white flowers. **Angel Mist Series** has plants available with purple, blue, white or bicolored flowers. '**Blue Pacific**' bears bicolored flowers of white and violet blue.

## Problems & Pests

Aphids and powdery mildew can cause trouble.

# Baby Blue-Eyes
## Five-Spot
### *Nemophila*

**Height:** 6–12" **Spread:** 12" **Flower color:** blue, white, purple

THESE LITTLE ANNUALS ARE SO CHARMING, BUT SO PICKY ABOUT their cultural conditions. If the truth be told, baby blue-eyes are much happier in cool, moist places, such as England or the northwestern U.S., but there is something about these plants that entices me. So, I have tried to find a place in my garden where they will thrive. For Ohio, a container is probably one of the best options. Be prepared to move it to a shadier, cooler location when the heat and humidity arrive in mid-summer. Baby blue-eyes will often perk up for a good autumn show.

*The genus name is from the Greek* nemos, *'glade,' and* philos, *'loving,' referring to the fact that baby blue-eyes prefer shady places.*

## Planting

**Seeding:** Direct sow around last frost date

**Planting out:** If necessary, after last frost date

**Spacing:** 8–12"

## Growing

Baby blue-eyes grow well in **full sun** or **partial shade**. The soil should be **fertile, moist** and **well drained**. Do not let the soil dry out completely. Shelter these plants from strong winds and avoid placing them near paths, where the tender foliage may be damaged by passersby.

These plants resent being transplanted and should be sown directly into the garden. They can be started indoors in peat pots or pellets in early spring if desired.

## Tips

Baby blue-eyes plants can be used as annual groundcovers or as edging for borders. They work well in mixed planters, hanging baskets and window boxes.

## Recommended

*N. maculata* (five-spot) is a low, mound-forming plant. It grows up to 12" tall, with an equal spread. The white flowers have purple veins, and each of the five petals has a single purple spot at the tip, giving the plant its common name.

*N. menziesii* (baby blue-eyes) is a low, spreading plant 6–10" tall and 12" wide. The flowers are blue with white centers. '**Pennie Black**' is a common cultivar. It has very dark purple flowers with silvery white edges.

'Pennie Black' (photos this page)

## Problems & Pests

Aphids and powdery mildew can cause problems.

*These plants may cease flowering during the hottest part of summer if they are allowed to completely dry out.*

# Baby's Breath
## Annual Baby's Breath
*Gypsophila*

**Height:** 10–36"  **Spread:** 12–24"  **Flower color:** white, pink, mauve

LIKE ITS PERENNIAL COUSIN, *GYPSOPHILA PANICULATA*, ANNUAL baby's breath provides a misty, 'see-through' effect in the garden. It is a wonderful annual to place around Oriental poppy *(Papaver orientale)*, which performs a disappearing act in June. As the poppy's foliage fades away, baby's breath takes center stage with its white to pink stars. And its shallow root system does not compete with the roots of the poppy. Baby's breath also makes a perfect cut flower. Its airy flower stems complement any plant, in or out of the garden.

## Planting

**Seeding:** Indoors in late winter; direct sow mid-spring to early summer

**Planting out:** Mid-spring

**Spacing:** 8–18"

## Growing

Baby's breath grows best in **full sun**. The soil should be of **poor fertility, light, sandy** and **alkaline**. This plant is drought tolerant; take care not to overwater because it does not grow well in wet soil. Don't space the seedlings too far apart because slightly crowded plants flower more profusely. Individual plants are short-lived, so sow seeds every week or two until early summer to encourage a longer blooming period.

## Tips

The clouds of flowers are ideal for rock gardens, rock walls, mixed containers or borders with bold-colored flowers. Baby's breath is native to the northeastern Mediterranean and looks very good in a Mediterranean-style garden.

## Recommended

*G. elegans* forms an upright mound of airy stems, foliage and flowers. The plant grows 12–24" tall. The flowers are usually white but may have pink or purple veining that gives a colored tinge. **'Covent Garden'** has very large, white flowers and grows to 20–36" tall.

*G. muralis* is a lower mounded species that flowers longer than *G. elegans*. The species is rarely grown, but the compact cultivar **'Gypsy Pink'** is quite common. It bears double or semi-double pink flowers and grows about 10–12" tall.

## Problems & Pests

Most common are fungal diseases that can be avoided by not overwatering and not handling plants when they are wet. Leafhoppers can infect baby's breath with aster yellows.

*G. elegans* (photos this page)

Gypsophila *comes from the words gypsum, or sulfate of lime, and* philos, *'loving,' referring to the plant's preference for chalky soils.*

# Bachelor's Button
## Cornflower, Blue-Bottle
### *Centaurea*

**Height:** 12–39" **Spread:** 6–24" **Flower color:** blue, purple, red, pink, white

NOTHING SHOUTS 'COTTAGE GARDEN' LOUDER THAN BACHELOR'S button. And few flowers have been cultivated for as long. This lovely annual has been noted in gardens as far back as the classical Greek civilization. The name bachelor's button supposedly originated from the practice of wearing one of these blooms to signal you were single. Furthermore, if the blossom was in good condition after being worn for 24 hours, it indicated that you would not be single for long. That's putting a lot of faith in a flower that hasn't been in water for a day!

### Planting

**Seeding:** Direct sow in mid-spring or start indoors in late winter; seed started indoors should be planted in peat pots or pellets to avoid disturbing the roots when transplanting

**Planting out:** Around last frost

**Spacing:** 12"

*The genus name,* Centaurea, *comes from Kentaurus, 'centaur,' because the mythical centaurs were said to nibble on bachelor's button to restore their vigor.*

## Growing

Bachelor's button does best in **full sun**. It prefers **fertile, moist, well-drained** soil but tolerates any soil. Light frost won't harm it. Shear spent flowers and old foliage in mid-summer for fresh growth. Deadhead to prolong blooming.

## Tips

Bachelor's button is a great filler plant in a mixed border or in a wild-flower or cottage-style garden. It is attractive in masses or small groups. Mix it with other plants—as the bachelor's button fades, the other plants can fill in the space it leaves. Seeds can be sown again in mid-summer and will provide flowers in fall, just when many summer plants begin to fade.

## Recommended

*C. cyanus* is an upright annual that grows 12–36" tall and spreads 6–24". The flowers are most often blue but can be shades of red, pink, violet or white. Plants in the **Boy Series** grow up to 39" tall and have large double flowers in many colors. '**Florence**' is a compact dwarf cultivar that grows 12–18" tall and has flowers in various colors. '**Frosty**' bears flowers in all colors, with white- or light-tipped petals. **Polka Dot Mix** bears double flowers in shades of blue, purple, red, pink or white on plants that grow about 18" tall.

## Problems & Pests

Aphids, downy mildew and powdery mildew may cause problems.

*C. cyanus* (photos this page)

*This plant grows wild in European grain fields, hence the alternative common name cornflower. Bachelor's button is also a common naturalized weed across most of the U.S.*

# Bacopa

*Sutera*

**Height:** 3–6"  **Spread:** 12–20"  **Flower color:** white, lavender

BACOPA IS ONE OF MY FAVORITE CONTAINER PLANTS. IT SNUGGLES under and around the stems of taller plants and eventually forms a solid carpet dotted with tiny white to pale lavender flowers. Eventually it drifts over pot edges and forms a waterfall of stars. I have tried using bacopa in the garden, but it does not like dry soils. It is almost impossible to keep it as moist as it needs to be during our summer droughts. So, plant it with other plants that prefer consistently moist soils. A lovely combination is the cultivar 'Snowflake' planted at the feet of 'Sensation,' a fragrant lavender miniature rose.

## Planting

**Seeding:** Not recommended

**Planting out:** Once soil has warmed

**Spacing:** 12"

## Growing

Bacopa grows well in **partial shade,** with protection from the hot afternoon sun. The soil should be of **average fertility, humus rich, moist** and **well drained.**

Don't allow this plant to dry out, or the leaves will quickly die. Cutting back dead growth may encourage new shoots to form.

'Olympic Gold' (above), 'Giant Snowflake' (below)

## Tips

Bacopa is a popular plant for hanging baskets, mixed containers and window boxes. It is not recommended as a bedding plant because it fizzles quickly when the weather gets hot, particularly if you forget to water. Plant it where you will see it every day and where it will be easy for you to water it.

## Recommended

*S. cordata* is a compact, trailing plant that bears small, white flowers all summer. **'Giant Snowflake'** is a more vigorous development of 'Snowflake.' **'Lavender Showers'** forms a dense mound of heart-shaped leaves with scalloped edges. It bears tiny, star-shaped, lavender flowers along its neat, trailing stems. **'Olympic Gold'** has white flowers and gold-variegated foliage. **'Snowflake,'** one of the first cultivars available, bears white flowers.

## Problems & Pests

Whiteflies and other small insects can become a real menace to this plant because the dense growth with tiny leaves makes a perfect hiding spot for them.

# Begonia

*Begonia*

**Height:** 6–24"  **Spread:** 6–24"  **Flower color:** pink, white, red, yellow, orange, bicolored or picotee; plant also grown for foliage

IF YOU ARE A FOLIAGE FANATIC, THEN BE PREPARED TO BECOME addicted to begonias. Rex begonia leaves can be pebbly, corrugated or smooth, and the colors can be subtle greens or flashy reds and silvers. It is difficult to keep track of the many forms. Curious forms are the easiest to remember; a good example is 'Escargot,' which spirals like its namesake. If flowers are more to your liking, search for the peony-flowered tuberous begonias. It is easy to become lost in their lush, deeply colored flowers. One of my favorite nursery stops is Baker's Acres in Alexandria, Ohio. They have as many as 60 begonia offerings.

## Planting

**Seeding:** Indoors in early winter

**Planting out:** Once soil has warmed

**Spacing:** According to spread of variety

## Growing

**Light** or **partial shade** is best, although some wax begonias tolerate sun if their soil is kept moist. The soil should be **fertile,** rich in **organic matter** and **well drained** with a **neutral or acidic** pH. Allow the soil to dry out slightly between waterings, particularly for tuberous begonias. Begonias love warm weather, so don't plant them before the soil warms in spring. If they sit in cold soil, they may become stunted and fail to thrive.

Begonias may be tricky to grow from seed. The tiny seeds can be mixed with a small quantity of fine sand before sowing to ensure a more even distribution of seeds. Keep the soil surface moist but not soggy, do not cover the seeds, and maintain daytime temperatures at 70°–80° F and night temperatures above 50° F. Begonias can be potted individually once they have three or four leaves and are large enough to handle.

Tubers can be purchased in early spring and started indoors. Plant them with the concave side up. The tubers of tuberous begonias can also be uprooted when the foliage dies back and stored in slightly moistened peat moss over winter. The tuber will sprout new shoots in late winter and can be potted for the following season.

*B. semperflorens*

*Many begonias have attractive, colorful foliage. Use the dark-leaved forms of wax begonias for splashes of contrasting color next to a gray-leaved* Helichrysum *or silver-leaved perennial* Lamium.

*B.* x *tuberhybrida* cultivar

B. *semperflorens* cultivar & *Buxus* (above),
'Escargot' (below)

Wax begonias can be dug out of the garden before the first frost and grown as houseplants in winter in a bright room.

## Tips

All begonias are useful for shaded garden beds and planters. The trailing tuberous varieties can be used in hanging baskets and along rock walls where the flowers will cascade over the edges. Wax begonias have a neat rounded habit that makes them particularly attractive as edging plants. They can also be paired with roses and geraniums in a front-yard bed for a formal look. Creative gardeners are using the rex begonias, with their dramatic foliage, as specimen plants in containers and beds.

## Recommended

*B.* **Rex Cultorum Hybrids** (rex begonias) are a group of plants developed from crosses between *B. rex* and other species. The plants grow 12–30" tall and 12–24" wide. They are grown for their dramatic, colorful foliage. These plants can also be grown as houseplants, and depending on the levels of light in your home the leaves will take on different colors. '**Colorvision**' is available from seed and provides plants with pink, red, bronze and white markings on green leaves. '**Escargot**' has brightly colored leaves that form an unusual spiral shape.

*B. semperflorens* (wax begonias) have pink, white, red or bicolored flowers and green, bronze, reddish or white-variegated foliage. The plants are 6–14" tall and 6–24" wide and require little maintenance. Plants in the **Ambassador Series** are heat tolerant and have dark green leaves and white, pink or red flowers. **Cocktail Series** plants are sun and heat tolerant and have bronzed leaves and red, pink or white flowers.

*B.* x *tuberhybrida* (tuberous begonias) are generally sold as tubers. The flowers come in many shades of red, pink, yellow, orange or white. They can also be picotee, with the petal margins colored differently than the rest of the petal. The plants grow 8–24" tall and wide. **Non-stop Series** begonias can be started from seed. The plants grow about 12" tall, with an equal spread; their double and semi-double flowers come in pink, yellow, orange, red and white. *B.* x *t. pendula* '**Chanson**' includes attractive pendulous begonias with flowers in many bright shades.

## Problems & Pests

Problems with stem rot and gray mold can occur from overwatering.

*B.* x *tuberhybrida* cultivar

*Wax begonias are ideal easy-care flowers because they are generally pest free and bloom all summer, even without deadheading.*

*B. semperflorens* cultivar

# Bells-of-Ireland
## Shell Flower, Lady-in-a-Bathroom
### *Moluccella*

**Height:** 24–36" **Spread:** 10" **Flower color:** green

YOU'D THINK THAT BECAUSE WE ALREADY HAVE SO MUCH GREEN in our gardens, we wouldn't be intrigued by green flowers. But bells-of-Ireland, with its lime green blooms, combines well with any color in a flowerbed or in an arrangement. This plant creates a strong vertical accent in the middle to the back of the garden, and it never fails to attract attention. Be careful, though: like some other members of the mint family, bells-of-Ireland is armed. Watch for the spines hiding on the edges of the sepals when you deadhead or when you create that special flower arrangement.

## Planting

**Seeding:** Indoors in mid-winter or direct sow in mid-spring

**Planting out:** After last frost

**Spacing:** 12"

## Growing

Bells-of-Ireland prefers **full sun** but tolerates partial shade. The soil should be of **average to good fertility, moist** and **well drained.**

Newly planted seeds need light to germinate. Press them into the soil surface, but leave them uncovered. It is best to direct sow these plants because they resent being transplanted, but they can be started indoors in peat pots or pellets.

The tall stems may need staking in windy locations.

## Tips

Use bells-of-Ireland at the back of a border, where the green spikes will create an interesting backdrop for more brightly colored flowers.

This plant is prone to self-seeding.

## Recommended

*M. laevis* is an upright plant that bears spikes of flowers with creamy white, inconspicuous petals. The most interesting feature is the large, green, shell-like cup (enlarged calyx) encircling each flower. The species is generally grown, and cultivars are rarely offered.

*The greenish 'bells' are actually enlarged calyces; the rest of the flower is very small and hidden inside.*

*Contrary to what the name implies, this plant is native to the Middle East, not to Ireland.*

# Bidens

*Bidens*

**Height:** 12–24" **Spread:** 12–24" or more **Flower color:** yellow

THERE IS ALWAYS A NEGATIVE AND A POSITIVE WAY TO LOOK AT a plant. Some might say bidens is unruly, but I prefer to say it has a rambling nature that shows well in a hanging basket or a large, tall container. Bidens' golden flowers blend well with blues and purples. An effective combination I saw in a public garden consisted of bidens planted in a copper urn that had oxidized to a beautiful verdigris finish: simple, but stunning.

### Planting

**Seeding:** Direct sow in late spring or start indoors in late winter

**Planting out:** After last frost

**Spacing:** 12–24"

## Growing

Bidens grows well in **full sun**. The soil should be **average to fertile, moist** and **well drained**.

If your bidens becomes lank and unruly in summer, shear it back lightly to encourage new growth and fall flowers.

## Tips

Bidens can be included in mixed borders, containers, hanging baskets and window boxes. Its fine foliage and attractive flowers make it useful for filling spaces between other plants.

## Recommended

*B. ferulifolia* is a bushy, mounding plant with fine, ferny foliage and bright yellow flowers. The cultivar **'Golden Goddess'** has even narrower foliage and larger flowers.

## Problems & Pests

Problems can occur with fungal diseases such as leaf spot, powdery mildew and rust.

B. ferulifolia

*This cheerful plant in the daisy family is always in flower and makes a wonderful annual groundcover.*

B. ferulifolia *is native to Arizona and Mexico, so it is well equipped to handle full sun and heat in Ohio gardens.*

B. ferulifolia & Calibrachoa 'Terracotta'

# Black-Eyed Susan
## Coneflower
*Rudbeckia*

**Height:** 8–36" or more  **Spread:** 12–18"  **Flower color:** yellow, orange, red, brown or sometimes bicolored; brown or green centers

IN A PUBLIC GARDEN, I ONCE SAW THE BLACK-EYED SUSAN CULTIVAR 'Irish Eyes' combined with red-hot poker (*Kniphofia* hybrid), spike gayfeather *(Liatris spicata)* and perennial salvia *(Salvia x sylvestris)*. I still remember vividly the way the vibrant swirl of gold, red and fuchsia was balanced by the salvia's cool blue. Black-eyed Susan is a short-lived perennial—so short it often lasts only one year—that has brightened up many spots in my garden. The cultivars 'Gloriosa' and 'Rustic Colors' bring glorious autumn colors into the garden with their deep gold, maroon and rust blooms.

## Planting

**Seeding:** Indoors in late winter; direct sow in mid-spring

**Planting out:** Late spring

**Spacing:** 18"

## Growing

Black-eyed Susan grows equally well in **full sun** or **partial shade**. The soil should be of **average fertility, humus rich, moist** and **well drained.** This plant tolerates heavy clay soil and hot weather. If it is growing in loose, moist soil, black-eyed Susan may reseed itself.

## Tips

Plant black-eyed Susan individually or in groups. Use it in beds and borders, large containers, meadow plantings and wildflower gardens. This plant will bloom well, even in the hottest part of the garden.

Keep cutting the flowers to promote more blooming. Black-eyed Susan makes a long-lasting vase flower.

*R. hirta* (above), 'Becky Mixed' (below)

'Cherokee Sunset' (above), 'Irish Eyes' (below)

*Black-eyed Susan and its cultivars make excellent additions to wildflower and natural gardens.*

*R. hirta* is a perennial that is grown as an annual. It is not worth trying to keep over winter because it grows and flowers quickly from seed.

## Recommended

*R. hirta* forms a bristly mound of foliage and bears bright yellow, daisy-like flowers with brown centers in summer and fall. **'Becky'** is a dwarf cultivar up to 12" tall, with large flowers in solid and mixed shades of yellow, orange, red and brown. **'Cherokee Sunset'** bears 3–4$^{1}/_{2}$" semi-double and double flowers in all colors. It is an All-America Selections winner for 2002. **'Gloriosa'** bears 6" single flowers in solid or bicolored shades of yellow, orange, bronze and gold. Plants grow up to 36" tall. **'Indian Summer'** has huge flowers, 6–10" across, on sturdy stems 36" tall or taller. **'Irish Eyes'** grows up to 30" tall and has

green-centered single blossoms.
**'Rustic Colors'** has flowers in
autumn colors. It grows 24–30" tall.
**'Toto'** is a dwarf cultivar that grows
8–12" tall, small enough for planters.

## Problems & Pests

Good air circulation around black-
eyed Susan plants will help prevent
fungal diseases such as powdery
mildew, downy mildew and rust.
Aphids can also cause problems
occasionally.

*With its hairy stems that are
difficult for insects to climb,
black-eyed Susan can act as a
'bug guard' near fields or houses.*

'Irish Eyes' (above), 'Gloriosa' (below)

# Black-Eyed Susan Vine

*Thunbergia*

**Height:** 5' or more  **Spread:** equal to height, if trained  **Flower color:** yellow, orange, violet blue or white, usually with dark centers

THESE BEAUTIFUL VINES HAVE NO FAMILIAL RELATIONSHIP WITH the black-eyed Susans (*Rudbeckia* species), but they do share an ability to brighten a space. If sited well and allowed to climb, *T. alata* decorates the garden with deep golden blooms. Its cousin, skyflower vine *(T. grandiflora),* cools the temperature in the garden with its true blue blooms. Find seed and start skyflower vine six to eight weeks before your last frost date because it tends to mature and bloom later
in the season.

## Planting

**Seeding:** Indoors in mid-winter; direct sow in mid-spring

**Planting out:** Late spring

**Spacing:** 12–18"

## Growing

Black-eyed Susan vines do well in **full sun, partial shade** or **light shade**. Grow in **fertile, moist, well-drained** soil that is high in **organic matter**. These vigorous vines may need to be trimmed back from time to time, particularly if they are brought inside for winter.

## Tips

Black-eyed Susan vines can be trained to twine up and around fences, walls, trees and shrubs. They are also attractive trailing down from the top of a rock garden or rock wall or growing in mixed containers and hanging baskets. Bring the plants into the house for winter, then return them to the garden the next spring—they are perennials treated as annuals.

To acclimatize the plants to the lower light levels indoors, gradually move them to more shaded locations. Keep in a bright room out of direct sunlight. The following spring, harden off the plants before moving them outdoors.

## Recommended

*T. alata* is a vigorous, twining climber. It bears yellow flowers, often with dark centers, in summer and fall. **Susie Series** plants are commonly available and bear large flowers in yellow, orange or white.

*T. grandiflora* (skyflower vine, blue trumpet vine) is a less commonly available species than *T. alata;* it is most often seen growing in greenhouses. It tends to bloom late, in early to mid-fall. This twining climber bears stunning, pale violet blue flowers. '**Alba**' has white flowers.

*These easy-care plants are rarely troubled by pests or diseases.*

*Black-eyed Susan vine makes an excellent hanging plant. The blooms are trumpet shaped, with the dark centers forming a tube.*

*T. alata* cultivar (above), *T. alata* (below)

# Blanket Flower

## *Gaillardia*

**Height:** 12–36" **Spread:** 12–24" **Flower color:** red, orange or yellow, often in combination

THIS NATIVE ANNUAL IS SURE TO TURN UP THE HEAT IN YOUR garden. The blooms are so richly colored, I'm surprised 'fire flower' hasn't been used as a common name. Annual blanket flower is one of the parents of the popular perennial blanket flower (*Gaillardia* x *grandiflora*) and has many of the same cultural needs. Don't pamper it, because too rich a soil will cause blanket flower to overgrow and flop. If you leave some of the seedheads on the plants at the end of the season, you may be rewarded with seedlings the next year.

*The multi-colored petals of Gaillardia (gay-lard-ee-a) flowers add a fiery glow to cottage gardens and meadow plantings.*

## Planting

**Seeding:** Indoors in late winter; direct sow in mid-spring

**Planting out:** Mid- to late spring

**Spacing:** 12"

## Growing

Blanket flower prefers **full sun**. The soil should be of **poor** or **average fertility, light, sandy** and **well drained**. The less water this plant receives, the better it will do. Don't cover the seeds, because they need light to germinate. They also require warm soil.

Deadhead to encourage more blooms.

## Tips

Blanket flower has an informal, sprawling habit that makes it a perfect addition to a casual cottage garden or mixed border. Because it is drought tolerant, it is well suited to exposed, sunny slopes, where it can help retain soil while more permanent plants grow in.

Make sure to place blanket flower in a location where it will not get watered with other plants.

## Recommended

*G. pulchella* forms a basal rosette of leaves. The daisy-like flowers are red with yellow tips. **Plume Series** plants have double flowerheads in vibrant shades of red or yellow. The series includes the popular cultivar 'Red Plume,' a dwarf plant that grows about 12" tall, with an equal spread, and blooms for a long time.

'Red Plume' (above), *G. pulchella* (below)

## Problems & Pests

Possible problems include leafhoppers, powdery mildew, aster yellows, rust and bacterial and fungal leaf spot. If you avoid overwatering, most problems will not become serious.

*This plant was named blanket flower because the vivid blossoms called to mind the colors in Navajo blankets.*

# Blood Flower
## Annual Butterflyweed, Swan Plant
*Asclepias*

---

**Height:** 2–6' **Spread:** 24–36" **Flower color:** red, orange, yellow, white, greenish white

SWAN PLANT *(A. PHYSOCARPA)* WAS INTRODUCED TO ME BY A friend who loves to discover unusual plants. It flowers continuously through the summer, and by early fall you will see blooms at the top of the plant and prickly, puffball seedpods developing lower down. Swan plant is no shrinking violet—it grew to 6' in my garden—but its size allowed me to easily watch the monarch butterflies hanging from the pendent flowers, sipping nectar. Blood flower *(A. curassavica)* is a bit smaller, but no less striking. And, like all its *Asclepias* relations, it is a butterfly magnet. Combine blood flower with other prairie plants and ornamental grasses.

### Planting

**Seeding:** Start indoors in mid-winter; soil temperature about 62° F

**Planting out:** Once frost danger has passed and soil has warmed

**Spacing:** 24–36"

## Growing

All blood flowers prefer **full sun**. The soil should be **average to fertile** and **well drained**. These plants are extremely drought tolerant.

In its native habitat, *A. curassavica* is considered to be a bit weedy because it readily self-sows. In a true Zone 5 winter, the seed may not survive, but it will make it through a warmer Zone 6 or 7 winter. *A. physocarpa* seed is less hardy and needs to be started indoors.

## Tips

These striking plants make an interesting accent in the center of a border. If grown in containers they can be moved indoors for the winter.

When overwintering these plants, give them a very bright location and a large space. Otherwise they will become stressed and more susceptible to pests and disease.

## Recommended

*A. curassavica* (blood flower) is a shrubby, upright plant 2–4' tall and about 24" in spread. It is actually a South American evergreen sub-shrub, but it can be treated as an annual in cooler climates. Clusters of red, orange or yellow flowers are produced from mid-summer to fall.

*A. physocarpa* (*Gomphocarpus physocarpus;* swan plant) is a tall, upright deciduous shrub native to southern Africa. It is treated as an annual in Ohio. It grows 3–6' tall and spreads about 36". In summer, pendulous clusters of white or greenish flowers are produced. The flowers are followed by prickly seedpods that

resemble swans, giving the plant its common name.

## Problems & Pests

Whiteflies can be a problem, but more so when plants are grown indoors. Aphids and mealybugs can also be problems.

*A. curassavica* (above), *A. physocarpa* (below)

# Browallia
## Amethyst Flower, Sapphire Flower
*Browallia*

**Height:** up to 8–18" **Spread:** up to 8–18" **Flower color:** purple, blue, white

HAVING A PREFERENCE FOR BLUE, I WAS IMMEDIATELY attracted to browallia. My first browallia was a houseplant. My second was in a hanging basket that somehow didn't make it into the house when the temperature dropped into the mid-30s. Like many of its relatives, including potatoes and tomatoes, this tender perennial is native to South America. Good drainage is essential, as is a consistently moist soil, so plants often do better grown in containers than in the ground.

### Planting

**Seeding:** Indoors in late winter. Do not cover the seeds, because they need light to germinate.

**Planting out:** Once soil has warmed

**Spacing:** 8–10"

## Growing

Browallia tolerates any light conditions from **full sun to full shade,** but flower production and color are best in partial shade. The soil should be **fertile** and **well drained.** Fertilize early in the season. Avoid using a fertilizer with a high percentage of nitrogen or you will get great foliage, but few flowers.

Browallia does not like the cold, so wait several weeks after the last frost before setting out the plants. Pinch tips often to encourage new growth and more blooms.

'White Troll' (above), *B. speciosa* (below)

## Tips

Grow browallia in mixed borders, mixed containers or hanging baskets. It can be brought indoors at the end of the season to be used as a houseplant during winter, or grown as a houseplant all year.

## Recommended

*B. speciosa* forms a bushy mound of foliage. This plant grows 8–18" tall with an equal or narrower spread and bears white, blue or purple flowers all summer. **Jingle Bells Series** includes **'Blue Bells'** and **'Silver Bells,'** which vary from 8" to 12" in both height and spread. **'Starlight'** forms a compact mound up to 8" high and wide. Its flowers may be light blue, bright blue, purple or white. **Troll Series** includes **'Blue Troll'** and **'White Troll,'** which are compact and bushy. They grow about 10" tall.

## Problems & Pests

Browallia is generally problem free. Whiteflies may cause some trouble.

# Calendula
## Pot Marigold, English Marigold
*Calendula*

**Height:** 10–24"  **Spread:** 8–20"  **Flower color:** cream, yellow, gold, orange, apricot

CALENDULA IS THE PERFECT ANNUAL. IT IS A RELATIVELY LOW-maintenance plant; it produces abundant seeds that can be shared with friends; its flowers look lovely cut for arrangements; and its seedlings sprout every year in places that need a bit of sunshine. This plant is so useful, I can't imagine a garden without it. For butterflies, it produces a seemingly endless supply of nectar. For people, the petals add a piquant note to green salads. Herbalists have made many claims for its curative powers, and few side effects have been recorded.

*Calendula flowers are popular kitchen herbs that can be added to stews for color or to salads for flavoring. They can also be brewed into an infusion that is useful as a wash for minor cuts and bruises.*

## Planting

**Seeding:** Direct sow in mid-spring; sow indoors a month or so earlier

**Planting out:** Mid-spring

**Spacing:** 8–10"

## Growing

Calendula does equally well in **full sun** or **partial shade.** It likes cool weather and can withstand a moderate frost. The soil should be of **average fertility** and **well drained.** Deadhead to prolong blooming and keep plants looking neat. If plants fade in summer heat, cut them back to 4–6" above the ground to promote new growth, or pull them up and seed new ones. Either method will provide a good fall display.

## Tips

This informal plant looks attractive in borders and mixed into the vegetable patch. It can also be used in mixed planters. Calendula is a cold-hardy annual and often continues flowering, even through a layer of snow, until the ground freezes completely.

Young plants are sometimes difficult to find in nurseries because calendula is so quick and easy to start from seed.

## Recommended

*C. officinalis* is a vigorous, tough, upright plant 12–24" tall, with a slightly lesser spread. It bears daisy-like, single or double flowers in a wide range of yellow and orange shades. **'Bon Bon'** is a dwarf plant that grows 10–12" tall and comes in a range of colors. **'Fiesta Gitana'**

('Gypsy Festival') is a dwarf plant with flowers in a range of colors. **'Pacific Beauty'** is larger, growing about 18" tall. It bears large flowers in varied colors. **'Pink Surprise'** bears pale orange and apricot flowers tinged with pink.

## Problems & Pests

Calendula plants are often trouble free, but they can have problems with aphids and whiteflies as well as smut, powdery mildew and fungal leaf spot. They usually continue to perform well even when they are afflicted with such problems.

*C. officinalis* cultivar (above), *C. officinalis* (below)

# California Poppy

*Eschscholzia*

**Height:** 8–18" **Spread:** 8–18" **Flower color:** orange, yellow, red; less commonly pink, cream

CALIFORNIA POPPIES ARE APTLY DESCRIBED AS THE SHIMMERING, fluttering apricot orange jewels of the west. They are available in other colors and in double-flowered forms, but the species is my favorite. California poppies graced the entrance beds at Inniswood Metro Gardens for years, but over time the population has decreased as the other plants in the bed have increased in size. California poppies are not fond of sharing space with plants that steal the sun. Plant them in open, sunny spaces and they will thrive.

## Planting

**Seeding:** Direct sow in early to mid-spring

**Spacing:** 6–12"

## Growing

California poppy prefers **full sun**. The soil should be of **poor** or **average fertility** and **well drained**. With too rich a soil, the growth will be lush and green but the plants will bear few, if any, flowers. This plant is drought tolerant once established.

Never start this plant indoors because it dislikes having its roots disturbed. California poppy will sprout quickly when planted directly in the garden. Sow in early spring for blooms in summer.

California poppy requires a lot of water for germination and development of young plants. Until they flower, provide the plants with regular and frequent watering. Once they begin flowering, they are more drought tolerant.

*E. californica* (photos this page)

## Tips

California poppy can be included in an annual border or annual planting in a cottage garden. This plant self-seeds wherever it is planted; it is perfect for naturalizing in a meadow garden or rock garden where it will come back year after year.

## Recommended

*E. californica* grows 8–18" tall and wide, forming a mound of delicate, feathery, blue-green foliage. It bears satiny orange or yellow flowers all summer. '**Ballerina**' has a mixture of colors and semi-double or double flowers. '**Chiffon**,' a compact plant up to 8", bears semi-double flowers in pink and apricot. '**Mission Bells**' bears ruffled, double and semi-double flowers in mixed and solid shades of orange, yellow, red, cream and pink. '**Thai Silk**' bears flowers in pink, red, yellow and orange with silky, wavy-edged petals. The compact plants grow 8–10" tall.

## Problems & Pests

California poppy generally has few pest problems, but fungi may cause trouble occasionally.

# Candytuft

*Iberis*

**Height:** 6–12" **Spread:** 8" or more **Flower color:** white, pink, purple, red

CANDYTUFT IS A FRAGRANT ANNUAL THAT WILL PERFUME AN entryway or a patio area. It resembles its perennial cousin, *Iberis sempervirens*, and looks like a more robust version of alyssum, to which it is also closely related. Like its cousins, candytuft provides a low carpet of color at the feet of other plants in the front of the garden. Annual candytuft is in bloom for a good part of the season provided it is deadheaded and placed in a sunny, but cooler, spot of the garden.

*If your candytuft seems to be blooming less often as summer progresses, trim it back lightly to promote new growth and more flowers.*

## Planting

**Seeding:** Indoors in late winter; outdoors around last frost

**Planting out:** After last frost

**Spacing:** 6"

## Growing

Candytuft prefers to grow in **full sun** or **partial shade**. Partial shade is best if it gets very hot in your garden. Like many species in the mustard family, candytuft dislikes heat; blooming will often slow down or decrease in July and August. The soil should be of **poor** or **average fertility, well drained** and have a **neutral** or **alkaline pH**.

Deadheading when the seeds begin to form will keep candytuft blooming, but do let some plants go to seed to guarantee repeat performances.

## Tips

This informal plant can be used on rock walls, in mixed containers or as edging for beds.

*I. umbellata* (photos this page)

## Recommended

*I. umbellata* (globe candytuft) has flowers in shades of pink, purple, red or white. The plant grows 6–12" tall and spreads 8" or more. '**Dwarf Fairy**' ('Dwarf Fairyland') is a compact plant that bears many flowers in a variety of pastel shades.

## Problems & Pests

Keep an eye open for slugs and snails. Caterpillars can also be a problem. In poorly drained soil, fungal problems may develop.

# Canterbury Bells
## Cup-and-Saucer Plant
*Campanula*

**Height:** 18–36"  **Spread:** 12"  **Flower color:** blue, purple, pink, white

CANTERBURY BELLS, KNOWN FOR ITS
deep blue bell-shaped flowers, does not fail
to meet a gardener's expectations. The two
different common names relate to two different flower forms. Canterbury bells has a
single flower form, while cup-and-
saucer plants have a double form. The
flowers have an heirloom look about
them, and are well suited to cottage
gardens and perennial
borders. Most of the
cultivars are true bien-
nials and remain in a veg-
etative state for their first
year of life. A few cultivars
have been chosen for their
shorter seed-to-bloom time; I
guess you could say that these
biennials have been 'annualized.'

## Planting

**Seeding:** Indoors in mid-winter or outdoors in spring in a sheltered location to flower the following summer

**Planting out:** Early spring

**Spacing:** 6–12"

## Growing

Canterbury bells prefers **full sun** but tolerates partial shade. The soil should be **fertile, moist** and **well drained.** This plant will not suffer if the weather cools or if there is a light frost.

When sowing, leave seeds uncovered because they require light for germination. Harden off in a cold frame or on a sheltered porch before planting out. Canterbury bells transplants easily, even when in full bloom.

Canterbury bells is actually a biennial treated as an annual. This is why the plants must be started so early in the year. Plants purchased in 3¹/₂" pots are usually too small to grow to flowering size the first year.

## Tips

Planted in small groups, Canterbury bells looks lovely in a border or rock garden. It also makes a good addition to a cottage garden or other informal garden where its habit of self-seeding can keep it popping up year after year. The tallest varieties produce good flowers for cutting. Use dwarf varieties in planters.

## Recommended

*C. medium* forms a basal rosette of foliage. The pink, blue, white or purple cup-shaped flowers are borne on

tall spikes. The plant grows 24–36" tall and spreads about 12". **'Bells of Holland'** is a dwarf cultivar about 18" tall. It has flowers in various colors. **'Champion'** is a true annual cultivar, flowering much sooner from seed than the species or many other cultivars. Blue or pink flowers are available. **'Russian Pink,'** an heirloom cultivar, was recently reintroduced. It is another true annual cultivar, and it bears light pink flowers.

## Problems & Pests

Occasional, but infrequent, problems with aphids, crown rot, leaf spot, powdery mildew and rust are possible.

*C. medium* (photos this page)

# Cape Marigold
## African Daisy
*Dimorphotheca*

**Height:** 12–18" **Spread:** 12" **Flower color:** white, orange, yellow or pink; often with brown, orange or purple centers

ANOTHER DAISY FROM AFRICA THAT COMES IN A VARIETY OF colors, cape marigold would be a good plant for a floral clock. Its blooms open mid-morning and close by late afternoon. During the day, the flowers follow the sun's movement across the sky. Contrast that with some of the evening primroses (*Oenothera* species) that open late afternoon and close by mid-morning, and you have a flower ballet.

*Take along your umbrella on days when the flowers of cape marigolds remain closed. The blooms will not open if rain is forecast.*

## Planting

**Seeding:** Indoors in early spring; direct sow after last frost

**Planting out:** After last frost

**Spacing:** 12"

## Growing

Cape marigolds like **full sun**. The soil should be **light, fertile** and **well drained**. These plants are drought resistant.

If growing cape marigolds from seed, water the young seedlings freely. Otherwise they will fail to thrive.

Cape marigolds do not grow well in rainy weather. Plant them under the eaves of the house, in window boxes or in raised beds to protect them from too much rain.

## Tips

Cape marigolds are most attractive when planted in groups or masses. Use them in beds and borders. The flowers close at night and on cloudy days, so although they can be cut for flower arrangements, they might close if the vase isn't getting enough light.

## Recommended

*D. pluvialis* (cape marigold; rain daisy) has white flowers with purple on the undersides and bases of the petals. **'Glistening White'** is a compact plant that bears large, pure white flowers with black centers.

*D.* **'Salmon Queen'** bears salmon and apricot pink flowers on plants that spread to about 18".

*D. sinuata* (star of the veldt) forms a 12–18" mound. It bears yellow,

orange, white or pink daisy-like flowers all summer. Cultivars with larger flowers are available.

*D.* **'Starshine'** is a low, mound-forming cultivar with shiny flowers in pink, orange, white or red, with yellow centers.

## Problems & Pests

Fungal problems are likely to occur in hot and wet locations. Dry, cool places produce healthy plants that are less susceptible to disease.

*D. pluvialis* (above), *D. sinuata* (below)

# Celosia
## Cockscomb, Woolflower
*Celosia*

**Height:** 10–36" **Spread:** usually equal to height **Flower color:** red, orange, gold, yellow, pink, purple

DEEPLY COLORED AND 'PETTABLE,' CELOSIA WAS ONE OF MY favorite flowers when I was a child. Memories often differ from present experience, but in this case it seems that celosias have become even more intensely colored over the years. The Century Series of the plume form are so bright that it is difficult to look at them for more than a moment. You can't help wondering if the color is true when you see them pictured in a catalog. I assure you, it is!

*To dry the plumes, pick the flowers when they are at their peak and hang them upside down in a cool, shaded place.*

## Planting

**Seeding:** Indoors in late winter; direct sow in mid- to late spring

**Planting out:** Once soil has warmed

**Spacing:** Depends on variety

## Growing

A sheltered spot in **full sun** is best. The soil should be **fertile** and **well drained** with plenty of **organic matter** worked in. Celosias like to be watered regularly.

It is preferable to start celosias directly in the garden. If you need to start them indoors, start the seeds in peat pots or pellets and plant them in the garden before they begin to flower. If left too long in pots, the plants will suffer stunted growth and won't be able to adapt to the garden. Keep seeds moist while they are germinating, and do not cover them.

Use the expected spread of the variety to determine the appropriate spacing. It will usually be between 6" and 18".

'Startrek' (above), Plumosa Group (below)

Plumosa Group (above & next page),
Cristata Group (below)

## Tips

Use celosias in borders and beds as well as in planters. The flowers make interesting additions to cut arrangements, either fresh or dried. A mass planting of plume celosia looks bright and cheerful in the garden. The popular crested varieties work well as accents and as cut flowers.

## Recommended

*C. argentea* is the species from which both the crested and plume-type cultivars have been developed. The species itself is never grown. **Cristata Group** (crested celosia) has the blooms that resemble brains or rooster combs. This group has many varieties and cultivars. '**Jewel Box**' bears flowers in red, pink, orange, yellow and gold on compact plants 10" tall. **Plumosa Group** (plume celosia) has feathery, plume-like blooms. This group also has many varieties and cultivars. '**Century**' has neat, much-branched plants up to 24" tall and 18" in spread, with flowers in many bright colors. '**Fairy Fountains**' (dwarf fairy fountains) is a compact plant, 12" tall, that bears long-lasting flowers in red, yellow and pink. Another interesting recent development from the species is '**Startrek**,' which has bright, pink-plumed flowers that radiate out from a central plume.

*C. spicata* '**Flamingo**' ('Flamingo Feather') grows about 36" tall and has spikes of pink or purple flowers that fade to white.

## Problems & Pests

Celosia plants may develop root rot if planted out too early or if overwatered when first planted out. Cool, wet weather is the biggest problem.

*The genus name* Celosia *is derived from the Greek* keleos, *'burning,' referring to the intensely colorful blooms.*

# Chilean Glory Flower

*Eccremocarpus*

**Height:** 10–15'  **Spread:** 12"  **Flower color:** orange-red

IF YOU HAVE NOTHING TO DO FOR AN AFTERNOON, CONSIDER sitting and watching Chilean glory flower grow. This is a bit of an exaggeration, but this plant does manage a notable 10 to 15 feet of growth in a season. Chilean glory flower is related to a major hummingbird attractor: trumpet creeper vine (*Campsis radicans*). I have not seen a specific reference to Chilean glory flower being used in hummingbird gardens, but its brightly colored tubular flowers look like hummingbird restaurant signs. I plan to test this theory next season.

## Planting

**Seeding:** Indoors in late winter, early spring

**Planting out:** After last frost date

**Spacing:** 12"

## Growing

Chilean glory flower requires **full sun.** This is a very fast-growing climbing vine. It grows vigorously in **light, well-drained, fertile** soil.

## Tips

This fast-growing, long-blooming annual must have something to grow on or against—walls, arbors, tree trunks or fences are perfect places.

## Recommended

*E. scaber* is a slender vine that becomes completely covered with long, orange-red, tubular flowers. The flower clusters are produced from late spring until fall. **Anglia Hybrids** offer a wider selection of flower colors including red, pink, orange and yellow. **Tresco Mix** enjoys hot locations; it bears flowers of yellow, pink or red.

## Problems & Pests

Spider mites and whiteflies can be a problem when this vine is growing indoors, but outdoors, this plant is relatively pest free.

*The genus name is from the Greek* ekkremus, *'hanging,' and* karpos *'fruit,' referring to the hanging pods of the plant.*

# China Aster

*Callistephus*

**Height:** 6–36"  **Spread:** 10–18"  **Flower color:** purple, blue, pink, red, white, peach, yellow

THERE ARE MANY SELECTIONS OF CHINA ASTER, AND THEY ALL seem to have one thing in common: the vivid and dense flowers cannot be ignored. One curious form that creates an interesting effect in the garden is the quilled petal, where each petal forms a tube. China aster is prized for its bountiful blooms, which develop all season provided you feed and water the plants adequately. I tend to relegate the taller forms to the cutting garden, but the smaller cultivars are charming at the front of the garden.

## Planting

**Seeding:** Indoors in late winter; direct sow after last frost

**Planting out:** Once soil has warmed

**Spacing:** 6–12"

## Growing

China aster prefers **full sun** but tolerates partial shade. The soil should be **fertile, evenly moist, well drained** and of **neutral** or **alkaline pH**. China asters are heavy feeders, so you will need to fertilize to get flowers like those you see in catalogs.

Start seeds in peat pots or peat pellets, because this plant doesn't like having its roots disturbed. China aster forms a shallow root system that dries out quickly during dry spells; mulch to conserve moisture.

## Tips

China aster puts on a bright display when planted in groups. The plants are available in three height groups: dwarf, medium and tall. Use dwarf and medium varieties as edging plants and the taller varieties for cut-flower arrangements. Tall varieties may require staking.

## Recommended

*C. chinensis* is the source of many varieties and cultivars. 'Comet' is an early-flowering cultivar, growing about 10" tall, with large, quilled double flowers in white, yellow, pink, purple, red or blue. 'Duchess' plants are wilt resistant. The sturdy stems, up to 24" tall, bear colorful flowers with petals that curve in towards the center. 'Meteor' has plants up to 36" tall. The large

flowers, up to 4" across, are bright red with yellow centers. 'Pot 'n' Patio' is a popular dwarf cultivar that has double flowers and grows 6–8" tall, with an equal spread. 'Princess' grows up to 24" tall and bears quilled, double or semi-double flowers in a wide range of colors.

## Problems & Pests

Wilt diseases and aster yellows can be prevented by planting China aster in different locations each year and by planting resistant varieties. Keep China aster away from calendula, which hosts potentially harmful insects and diseases.

*C. chinensis* cultivars (photos this page)

# Chinese Forget-Me-Not

*Cynoglossum*

**Height:** 12–24" **Spread:** up to 12" **Flower color:** blue, sometimes pink or white

IF YOU WANT THE EFFECT OF FORGET-ME-NOTS (*MYOSOTIS* species), but you have a drier site, consider using Chinese forget-me-nots. Just understand that if you decide that you don't want these plants anymore, it may take a season or two to get rid of them. For years Chinese forget-me-nots provided a beautiful carpet under shrubs in the herb garden at Inniswood Metro Gardens. When it was decided to change the design, the little plants made sure we couldn't forget them. After three years, stray seedlings still pop up.

*The genus name comes from the Greek* kyon, *'dog,' and* glossum, *'tongue,' referring to the shape of the leaves.*

## Planting

**Seeding:** Indoors in early spring; direct sow in late spring

**Planting out:** Around last frost

**Spacing:** 12"

## Growing

Chinese forget-me-not prefers **full sun** or **partial shade**. The soil should be of **average fertility, moist** and **well drained**. A heavy clay or overly fertile soil will cause floppy, unattractive growth.

## Tips

Chinese forget-me-not can be used in difficult areas. The foliage is not exceptionally attractive, and the plants look best planted in masses or used to fill in the space under shrubs and other tall border plants.

This plant readily self-seeds and may return for many seasons. Be careful that it doesn't overtake your garden. Removing the flowerheads right before they seed will keep the self-seeding tendencies under control.

## Recommended

*C. amabile* forms an upright plant that branches strongly. It bears bright blue or sometimes white or pink flowers in small clusters. '**Blue Showers**' grows about 24" tall and bears attractive, light blue flowers. '**Firmament**' ('Firmament Blue') is a compact variety, about 12–18" tall, with hairy gray leaves. The pendulous flowers are sky blue.

## Problems & Pests

This plant is subject to root and stem rot and mildew, problems that can be avoided by not overwatering.

# Cleome
## Spider Flower
*Cleome*

**Height:** 1–5'  **Spread:** 18–36"  **Flower color:** pink, rose, violet, white

IF YOU ARE LOOKING FOR A BOLD statement in your garden, consider using cleome. This plant is attractive in flower and in seed, and it produces both in abundance. I have friends who say they have had many seedlings in spring, but I have not had their success—perhaps I cultivate my soil too much. One of my favorite combinations is *Cleome* 'Rose Queen,' *Salvia farinacea* 'Victoria,' and *Artemisia* 'Silver Brocade.' The combination of rose, deep blue and silver is very calming.

*'Spider flower' is another name for cleome, but 'hummingbird flower' might be more appropriate. These plants bloom through to fall, providing nectar for the tiny birds after many other flowers have finished blooming.*

## Planting

**Seeding:** Indoors in late winter; direct sow in spring

**Planting out:** After last frost

**Spacing:** 18–30"

## Growing

Cleomes prefer **full sun** but tolerate partial shade. Any kind of soil will do fine. Mix in plenty of **organic matter** to help the soil retain moisture. These plants are drought tolerant but look and perform better if watered regularly. Don't water them excessively or they will become leggy. Chill the seeds overnight prior to planting.

Pinch out the center of a cleome plant when transplanting, and it will branch out to produce up to a dozen blooms.

*C. hassleriana* (photos this page)

'Helen Campbell' (above)

Deadhead to prolong the blooming period and to minimize the plants' prolific self-sowing. Self-sown seedlings will start coming up almost as soon as the seeds hit the ground and can become invasive. Fortunately, the new plants are very distinctive and can be spotted poking up where they don't belong, making them easy to pull up while they are still young. Flowers of self-sown seedlings will most likely revert to purple, the original species' color.

## Tips

Cleome can be planted in groups at the back of a border. These plants are also effective in the center of an island bed; use lower-growing plants around the edges to hide the leafless lower stems of cleome.

Be careful when handling these plants because they have nasty barbs along the stems.

## Recommended

*C. hassleriana* is a tall, upright plant with strong, supple, thorny stems. It grows up to 5' tall. The foliage and flowers of this plant have a strong, but not unpleasant, scent. **'Helen Campbell'** has white flowers. **Royal Queen Series** has flowers in all colors, available by individual color or a mix of colors. The varieties are named by their color; e.g., **'Cherry Queen,' 'Rose Queen'** and **'Violet Queen.'** Plants in this series resist fading. **'Sparkler Blush'** is a dwarf cultivar that grows up to 3' tall. It bears pink flowers that fade to white.

*C. serrulata* (Rocky Mountain bee plant) is native to western North

America. It is rarely available commercially, but the dwarf cultivar 'Solo' is available to be grown from seed. It grows 12–18" tall and bears 2–3" pink and white blooms. This plant is thornless.

## Problems & Pests

Aphids may be a problem.

*The flowers can be cut for fresh arrangements, although the plants have an unusual odor that is noticeable up close. You can also try adding the seedpods to dried arrangements.*

*C. hassleriana* with *Nicotiana, Pelargonium & Impatiens*

# Climbing Snapdragon
## Twining Snapdragon
### *Asarina (Maurandya)*

**Height:** 18"–6'  **Spread:** equal to height, as trained  **Flower color:** purple, pink, blue, white, red

CLIMBING SNAPDRAGONS ARE CHARMING ADDITIONS TO A BIRD garden. Hummingbirds are known to prefer hot, bright colors, but these blue and purple flowers are also enticing invitations to dine. These tender perennials (Zones 9–10) will live for a long time in a container if they're brought into a cool room that has good indirect light. Do not allow the soil to freeze. The smaller *Asarina purpusii* is easier to overwinter. An option for overwintering the larger *A. scandens* is to start cuttings of the mature plant in late summer and overwinter those instead.

## Planting

**Seeding:** Direct sow in warm soil; start indoors in early spring

**Planting out:** After danger of frost

**Spacing:** 24"

## Growing

Climbing snapdragons grow well in **full sun, partial shade** or **light shade.** The soil should be **average to fertile, moist** and **well drained.** The leaves may scorch in hot afternoon sun. These climbers need a trellis or other frame to twine their tendrils around as they climb.

## Tips

Climbing snapdragons can be grown up a trellis or other structure. They look great in containers, where they can trail over the edge or grow up a wire frame. They can also be planted in a border where they will trail along the ground and over any objects they encounter.

## Recommended

*A. purpusii (M. purpusii)* is an attractive climbing plant. It grows 18–24" tall and bears purple, pink or white flowers. **'Victoria Falls'** is a trailing cultivar that bears many flowers in dark pink and is useful in hanging baskets.

*A. scandens (A. erubescens)* is a vigorous climber that flowers quickly from seed and continues to flower until the first hard frost. It grows up to 6' tall, or taller. It bears pink, white, red, purple or blue flowers. **Jewel Mix** bears flowers in a variety of colors. **'Joan Lorraine'** has purple flowers with white throats.

*A. purpusii*

*These plants are related to snapdragons but lack the hinged part of the flower that allows the dragon's mouth to be opened.*

## Problems & Pests

Climbing snapdragons rarely suffer from any problems.

# Coleus

*Solenostemon (Coleus)*

**Height:** 6–36" or more  **Spread:** usually equal to height  **Flower color:** light purple; plant grown for foliage

THERE IS A COLEUS FOR EVERYONE. IF YOU DON'T LIKE THE BRASH yellows, oranges and reds of many of the coleus, maybe you will be seduced by the deep maroon and rose selections. Chris Baker of Bakers Acres Nursery offers many cultivars, adding and subtracting every year. Every spring I feel like a kid in a candy shop and often buy more than I had planned. Fortunately, coleus are excellent container plants, and there is always room for another pot in the garden.

## Planting

**Seeding:** Indoors in winter

**Planting out:** Once soil has warmed

**Spacing:** 12"

## Growing

Seed-grown coleus prefers to grow in **light** or **partial shade** but tolerates full shade if the shade isn't too dense and full sun if the plants are watered regularly. Cultivars propagated from cuttings thrive in **full sun** to **partial shade**. The soil for all coleus should be of **rich to average fertility, humus rich, moist** and **well drained**.

Place the seeds in a refrigerator for one or two days before planting them on the soil surface; the cold temperatures will assist in breaking the seeds' dormancy. They need light to germinate. Seedlings will be green at first, but leaf variegation will develop as the plants mature.

*Coleus can be trained to grow into a standard (tree) form. Pinch off the lower leaves and side branches as they grow to create a long bare stem with leaves only on the upper half. Once the plant reaches the desired height, pinch from the top to create a bushy rounded crown.*

Coleus is easy to propagate from stem cuttings, and in doing so you can ensure that you have a group of plants with the same leaf markings, shapes or colors. As your seedlings develop, decide which you like best, and when they are about three pairs of leaves high, pinch off the tip. The plants will begin to branch out.

Pinch all the tips off regularly as the branches grow. This process will produce a very bushy plant from which you will be able to take a large number of cuttings. The cuttings should be about three leaf pairs long. Make the cut just below a leaf pair, and then remove the two bottom leaves. Plant the cuttings in pots filled with a soil mix intended for starting seeds. Keep the soil moist but not soggy. The plants should develop roots within a couple of weeks.

## Tips

The bold, colorful foliage makes coleus dramatic when the plants are grouped together as edging plants or in beds, borders or mixed containers. Coleus can also be grown indoors as a houseplant in a bright room.

When flower buds develop, it is best to pinch them off, because the plants tend to stretch out and become less attractive after they flower.

## Recommended

*S. scutellarioides* (*Coleus blumei* var. *verschaffeltii*) forms a bushy mound of foliage. The leaf edges range from slightly toothed to very ruffled. The leaves are usually multi-colored with shades ranging from pale greenish yellow to deep purple-black. The size

may be 6–36", depending on the cultivar, and the spread is usually equal to the height. Dozens of cultivars are available, but many cannot be started from seed. The following cultivars can be started from seed: those in the **Dragon Series,** with bright yellow-green margins around variably colored leaves; '**Garnet Robe,**' with a cascading habit and dark wine red leaves edged with yellow-green; '**Molten Lava,**' with dark red leaves; '**Palisandra,**' with velvety, purple-black foliage; '**Scarlet Poncho,**' with wine red leaves edged with yellow-green; and the **Wizard Series,** with variegated foliage on compact plants.

## Problems & Pests

Mealybugs, scale insects, aphids and whiteflies can cause occasional trouble.

*Although coleus is a member of the mint family, with the characteristic square stems, it has none of the enjoyable culinary or aromatic qualities.*

# Coreopsis

*Coreopsis*

**Height:** 8"–4' **Spread:** 8–18" **Flower color:** yellow, red, orange, brown

THE ANNUAL COREOPSIS LOOKS LIKE A DELICATE VERSION OF THE perennial blanket flower (*Gaillardia* x *grandiflora*), and like its cousin, blooms throughout the season. It is often included in wildflower mixes where its yellow flowers banded with red-orange add a cheery note to wildflower or cottage gardens. My preference is to grow the shorter cultivars because the stems tend to be a bit weak, and it is not unusual to find the taller cultivars taking a rest on the ground.

## Planting

**Seeding:** Indoors in mid-winter; direct sow after last frost

**Planting out:** After last frost

**Spacing:** 8–12"

## Growing

Coreopsis plants prefer **full sun** and will often become stretched and floppy in partial shade. The soil should be of **average to rich fertility, light** and **well drained**. Poor soil is also tolerated but with somewhat reduced flowering. Good drainage is the most important factor for these drought-tolerant plants.

## Tips

Try coreopsis in front of a rustic wooden fence or repeating in clusters in a bed of perennials. These plants make a beautiful color combination planted with deep purple coral bells or royal purple heliotrope. Effective in naturalized meadow plantings, coreopsis can also be used in informal beds and borders where they will flower all season if deadheaded regularly. These plants also produce lovely cut flowers.

Coreopsis plants can be blown over or have their stems broken during heavy rain or high winds. The fine foliage isn't dense enough to hide tomato or peony cages, so insert twiggy branches for the seedlings to grow between for support. In very windy spots, it is best to use the dwarf forms of coreopsis.

## Recommended

*C. tinctoria* forms a clump of basal leaves and tall, branching stems with

just a few leaves. It grows up to 4' tall and spreads up to 18". The flowers are usually bright yellow with dark red bands at the petal bases; flowers in red, orange or brown are also possible. Dwarf cultivars that grow about 8–12" tall are available.

## Problems & Pests

Slugs, snails and fungal diseases can be problems.

*Self-seeding is common with these plants, so they may pop up from year to year in the same area if left to their own devices.*

# Cosmos

*Cosmos*

**Height:** 1–7' **Spread:** 12–18" **Flower color:** white, yellow, gold, orange, shades of pink and of red

I AM OFTEN ASKED, 'WHAT IS THAT WILLOWY DAISY PLANTED IN the median of the freeway?' After a brief description it is easy to identify the mystery plant as cosmos. Unfortunately many of these stands have died out, but their appearance on Ohio freeways helped to make them a popular annual. The flower colors are deeply saturated and provide nectar for various butterflies. If you are looking for something different, search out plants or seeds of the Sea Shells Series. Their fluted petals add an interesting texture to the garden and the flower vase. Also look for the chocolate cosmos which, on a hot day, does smell like chocolate.

*The name* Cosmos *is from Greek and means 'harmony' or 'order.'*

## Planting

**Seeding:** Indoors in late winter; direct sow after soil has warmed

**Planting out:** After last frost

**Spacing:** 12–18"

## Growing

Cosmos like **full sun**. The soil should be of **poor or average fertility** and **well drained**. Cosmos are drought tolerant. Overfertilizing and over-watering can reduce the number of flowers produced. Yellow cosmos (*C. sulphureus*) will do better if sown directly in the garden. Keep faded blooms cut to encourage more buds. Often, these plants reseed them-selves.

Cosmos plants are likely to need staking but are difficult to stake. If you want to avoid staking, plant cos-mos in a sheltered location or against a fence. You could also grow

*C. bipinnatus* (photos this page)

*Cut flowers of cosmos make lovely, long-lasting fillers in arrangements.*

*C. atrosanguineus* (above), *C. bipinnatus* (below)

shorter varieties. If staking can't be avoided, push twiggy branches into the ground when the plants are young and allow them to grow up between the branches. The branches will be hidden by the mature plants.

## Tips

Cosmos are attractive in cottage gardens, at the back of a border or mass planted in an informal bed or border.

## Recommended

*C. atrosanguineus* (chocolate cosmos) has recently become popular among annual connoisseurs for its fragrant, deep maroon flowers that some claim smell like chocolate. The plant is upright, growing to 30" tall, but tends to flop over a bit when the stem gets too long.

*C. bipinnatus* (annual cosmos) has many cultivars. The flowers come in magenta, rose, pink or white, usually with yellow centers. Old varieties grow 3–6' tall, while some of the newer cultivars grow 12–36" tall. **'Daydream'** has white flowers flushed with pink at the petal bases. It grows up to 5' tall. **'Psyche'** bears large, showy, semi-double flowers in pink, white and red. **Sea Shells Series** has flowers in all colors and petals that are rolled into tubes. It grows up to 42" tall. **'Sensation'** bears large, white or pink flowers and grows up to 4' tall. **Sonata Series** has red, pink or white flowers on compact plants up to 24" tall.

*C. sulphureus* (yellow cosmos) has gold, orange, scarlet and yellow flowers. Old varieties grow 7' tall, and new varieties grow 1–4' tall.

'**Klondike**' is a compact cultivar about 12–24" tall. Its single or semi-double flowers are bright yellow or orange-red. **Ladybird Series** has compact dwarf plants, 12–14" tall, that rarely need staking. The foliage is not as feathered as it is in other cultivars.

## Problems & Pests

Cosmos rarely have any problems, but watch for wilt, aster yellows, powdery mildew and aphids.

*C. sulphureus* (above), *C. bipinnatus* (below)

# Creeping Zinnia
*Sanvitalia*

**Height:** 4–8" **Spread:** 12–18" **Flower color:** yellow or orange; dark brown or purple centers

IT SEEMS THAT WE JUST CAN'T GET ENOUGH OF MINIATURES. While strolling through a garden center I spied—and bought—this charming little daisy in a hanging basket. It demanded much less care than my impatiens basket and earned a return visit to my garden the following year. It seems to prefer living in a container rather than in the ground, and this may be because it needs very good drainage. Creeping zinnia is very attractive at the feet of scented geraniums and *Plectranthus* species.

## Planting

**Seeding:** Direct sow in mid-spring

**Spacing:** 12"

## Growing

Creeping zinnia prefers **full sun** although protection from the afternoon sun is beneficial during a hot summer. The soil should be of **average fertility, light, sandy** and very **well drained**.

Do not cover the seeds when you sow them, because they need light to germinate.

## Tips

Use creeping zinnia as an annual groundcover or edging plant. It is also dramatic in hanging baskets and in mixed containers.

Creeping zinnia is one of the easiest annuals to grow. It is also one of the easiest to damage with too much care; overwatering and overfertilizing can quickly kill it.

## Recommended

*S. procumbens* forms a low mat of foliage up to 8" tall. Small yellow or orange, daisy-like flowers with dark centers are borne from summer until long into fall. 'Sprite' is a mounding plant that has yellow-orange flowers with dark centers. 'Yellow Carpet' is a low-growing dwarf variety up to 4" tall and 18" wide. It has bright yellow flowers with dark centers.

*The less you do for it, the better this flowering plant will look.*

## Problems & Pests

Keep creeping zinnia from getting hit by a sprinkler system, or you'll have mildew and fungal problems.

*S. procumbens* (photos this page)

# Cup Flower

*Nierembergia*

**Height:** 6–12"  **Spread:** 6–12"  **Flower color:** blue, purple, white; yellow centers

THE FIRST YEAR I PLANTED IT, CUP FLOWER SURPRISED ME BY surviving a mild winter. But, alas, it did not survive the next. Cup flower prefers a mild summer, too—the wilting that I thought was from lack of water was actually a response to high temperatures. Unknowingly, I watered a few plants to death and learned that wilting is not always a sign of water need. The violet flowers of 'Purple Robe' combine beautifully with the perennial *Coreopsis* 'Moonbeam' and the silvery foliage of the perennial cheddar pinks (*Dianthus gratianopolitanus*).

## Planting

**Seeding:** Indoors in mid-winter

**Planting out:** Spring

**Spacing:** 6–12"

## Growing

Cup flower grows well in **full sun** or **partial shade**. It does best in the cooler part of the garden where there is protection from the afternoon sun. The soil should be of **average fertility, moist** and **well drained**. Fertilize little, if at all.

Cup flower is a perennial used as an annual. During a mild year, cup flower may survive winter. Unfortunately it may also suffer during the heat of summer. If your plant survives winter, take it as a bonus. However, it is often easier to start new plants each year than to overwinter mature plants.

## Tips

Use cup flower as a groundcover, for edging beds and borders, and for rock gardens, rock walls, containers and hanging baskets. It grows best when summers are cool, and it can withstand a light frost.

## Recommended

*N. hippomanica* (*N. caerulea*) forms a small mound of foliage. This plant bears delicate, cup-shaped flowers in lavender blue with yellow centers. **'Mont Blanc'** has white flowers with yellow centers. **'Purple Robe'** has deep purple flowers with golden eyes.

## Problems & Pests

Slugs and snails are likely to be the worst problems for this plant. Because cup flower is susceptible to tobacco mosaic virus, don't plant it near any flowering tobacco or tomato plants.

'Mont Blanc' (photos this page)

*The species name* hippomanica *is from the Greek and means 'drives horses crazy.' Whether they went crazy because they loved to eat it or from actually eating the plant is unclear.*

# Dahlberg Daisy
## Golden Fleece
### *Thymophylla*

**Height:** 6–12"  **Spread:** 12"  **Flower color:** yellow, less commonly orange

THIS DIMINUTIVE DAISY HAS AN IDENTITY CRISIS—IT CAN'T decide if it is an annual, a biennial or a short-lived perennial. I suspect it depends on the weather conditions, and somehow, Dahlberg daisy 'chooses' the best strategy for seed production. That aside, I have been most successful growing this plant in a container. Dahlberg daisy is not fond of Ohio's high heat and humidity, so if I happen to notice that my plants are suffering, I move them into a shadier, cooler part of the garden. An added bonus of growing Dahlberg daisy in a container is that it is closer to your nose, allowing you to enjoy its fragrant leaves and flowers.

## Planting

**Seeding:** Indoors in mid-winter; direct sow in spring

**Planting out:** After last frost

**Spacing:** 8–12"

## Growing

Plant Dahlberg daisy in **full sun**. Any **well-drained** soil is suitable, although soil of **poor or average fertility** is preferred. Dahlberg daisy prefers cool summers. In hot climates, it flowers in spring or late summer and fall.

Direct-sown plants may not flower until quite late in summer. For earlier blooms, start the seeds indoors. Don't cover the seeds, because they require light to germinate. Dahlberg daisy may self-sow and reappear each year. Trimming your plants back when flowering seems to be slowing will encourage new growth and more blooms.

## Tips

This attractive plant can be used along the edges of borders, along the tops of rock walls, or in hanging baskets or mixed containers. In any location where it can cascade over and trail down an edge, Dahlberg daisy will look wonderful.

## Recommended

*T. tenuiloba* (*Dyssodia tenuiloba*) forms a mound of ferny foliage. It produces many bright yellow, daisy-like flowers from spring until the summer heat causes it to fade. Trim it back once the flowers fade, and it may revive in late summer as the weather cools.

*Dahlberg daisy has fragrant foliage that some people compare to a lemon-thyme scent, perhaps the origin of the genus name* Thymophylla, *'thyme-leaf.'*

# Dahlia

*Dahlia*

**Height:** 8"–5' **Spread:** 8–18" **Flower color:** purple, pink, white, yellow, orange, red, bicolored

I HAVE RECENTLY JOINED THE RANKS OF CAPTIVATED DAHLIA growers. With their many forms—20 according to the American Dahlia Society (www.dahlia.org)—and color options, it will be awhile before I run out of dahlias to try. Their main time of show is late summer through fall, but this can be delayed if the summer is too hot and dry. Many dahlias have attractive foliage. A current favorite is the heirloom 'Bishop of Llandaff,' which has maroon foliage and the richest red-orange, single flowers I have ever seen. It grew up through the bronze fennel in my side garden; the combination was electric!

## Planting

**Seeding:** Indoors in mid- to late winter; direct sow in spring

**Planting out:** After last frost

**Spacing:** 12"

## Growing

Dahlias prefer **full sun**. The soil should be **fertile**, rich in **organic matter, moist** and **well drained**. All dahlias are tender tuberous perennials treated as annuals. Tubers can be purchased and started early indoors. The tubers can also be lifted in fall and stored over winter in slightly moist peat moss. Pot them and keep them in a bright room when they start sprouting in mid- to late winter.

If there is a particular size, color or form of dahlia that you want, it is best to start it from tubers of that type. Seed-grown dahlias show a great deal of variation in color and form because the seed is generally sold in mixed packages.

*Dahlia flowers are categorized by size, from giants with blooms more than 10" in diameter to mignons with blooms up to 2" in diameter. They are also categorized by flower type—for example, peony, formal and informal decorative, semi-cactus and waterlily.*

In order to keep dahlias blooming and attractive, it is essential to remove the spent blooms.

## Tips

Dahlias make attractive, colorful additions to a mixed border. The smaller varieties make good edging plants and the larger ones make good replacement plants for shrubs. Varieties with unusual or interesting flowers are attractive specimen plants.

## Recommended

Of the many dahlia hybrids, most must be grown from tubers but a few can be started from seed with good results. Examples of seed-started dahlias include '**Figaro,**' which forms a round, compact plant 12–16" tall. The flowers are small, double or semi-double, come in a wide variety of colors, and grow and flower quickly. This plant looks very good grouped in a border or in containers. '**Harlequin**' forms compact

Mixed cutting bed

plants that flower quickly from seed. Flowers are solid or bicolored, single or semi-double in many shades. Many hybrid seeds are sold in mixed packets based on flower shape; for example, collarette, decorative or peony flowered. Tubers of specific types and colors can be purchased in late winter and early spring.

## Problems & Pests

Dahlias may encounter a few problems: aphids, powdery mildew and slugs are the most likely. If a worse problem afflicts your dahlias, it may be best to destroy the infected plants and start over.

*Dahlia cultivars span a vast array of colors, sizes and flower forms, but breeders have yet to develop true blue, scented and frost-hardy varieties.*

*In the 18th century, the first European breeders of these Mexican plants were more interested in them as a possible food source. The blooms were thought to be unexceptional.*

Informal decorative type

Semi-cactus type

Formal decorative type

Peony type

# Diascia
## Twinspur
### *Diascia*

**Height:** 8–12"  **Spread:** 20"  **Flower color:** shades of pink

DIASCIA IS LISTED AS BEING HARDY TO ZONES 7 AND HIGHER SO is treated as an annual in Ohio. However, a friend has grown it and carried it over for two winters. These were warmer winters, approximately Zone 6 instead of Zone 5, but this means that diascia may be what we hopefully call a 'marginal perennial.' As with many plants from South Africa, the flower form of diascia is different from that of most plants from the northern hemisphere. Its twin-spurred nectaries and open snap-dragon form make it an intriguing addition to the garden. It will be interesting to observe which Ohio insects try to pollinate this plant.

## Planting

**Seeding:** Indoors in spring

**Planting out:** After the last frost

**Spacing:** 18"

## Growing

Diascias prefer **full sun** but enjoy protection from the afternoon sun when the weather is hot and humid. The soil should be **fertile, moist** and **well drained.** Diascias are generally frost hardy and bloom well into fall.

*D. barberae*

These plants don't thrive in high humidity and heat. Plants may fade during the hottest part of summer but will revive and produce flowers as temperatures drop in fall. Diascias are tender perennials treated as annuals in most of North America.

Deadheading will keep the blooms coming, and if flowering becomes sparse in searing summer heat, shearing will encourage new growth and a fresh flush of blooms when the weather cools.

## Tips

Diascias are attractive in a rock garden or mass planted in a border. Pinch tips of plants to increase bushiness.

## Recommended

*D. barberae* is a low-growing plant that bears loose spikes of pink flowers from mid-summer to frost. **'Blackthorn Apricot'** has apricot-colored flowers and flowerheads that point downwards. **'Pink Queen'** has light, shimmery pink flowers on long, slender stalks.

*D.* **'Coral Belle'** is a quick-growing hybrid that forms a dense mound of bright green foliage. The flowers are a delicate coral pink.

*D.* **'Strawberry Sundae'** is a fairly compact plant with trailing stems and bright pink flowers.

## Problems & Pests

Watch out for snails and slugs.

'Strawberry Sundae'

# Dusty Miller

*Senecio*

**Height:** 12–24" **Spread:** equal to height or slightly narrower
**Flower color:** yellow to cream; plant grown for silvery foliage

SILVER IS THE ULTIMATE BLENDER. IT ENHANCES ANY COLOR AND
tempers clashing hues. Dusty miller has become one of the most popular
silver plants not only because of its color but also because of its soft and lacy
texture. Dusty miller is also a valuable plant to use in crafts. The leaves, when
dried or pressed, retain their soft, silvery appearance. They are welcome
additions to potpourris and add a touch of elegance to homemade cards.
Here in central Ohio dusty miller is often combined with red-flowered
plants to represent Ohio State's colors: scarlet and gray.

## Planting

**Seeding:** Indoors in mid-winter

**Planting out:** Spring

**Spacing:** 12"

## Growing

Dusty miller prefers **full sun** but tolerates light shade. The soil should be of **average fertility** and **well drained**.

## Tips

The soft, silvery, lacy leaves of this plant are its main feature, and it is used primarily as an edging plant. It is also used in beds, borders and containers. The silvery foliage makes a good backdrop to show off the brightly colored flowers of other plants.

Pinch off the flowers before they bloom. They aren't showy and steal energy that would otherwise go to growing more foliage.

## Recommended

*S. cineraria* is a tender shrub that forms a mound of fuzzy, silvery gray, lobed or finely divided foliage. Many cultivars have been developed with impressive foliage colors and shapes. '**Cirrus**' has lobed, silvery green or white foliage. '**Silver Dust**' has deeply lobed, silvery white foliage. '**Silver Lace**' has delicate, silvery white foliage that glows in the moonlight.

*Mix dusty miller with geraniums, begonias or celosias to really bring out the vibrant colors of these flowers.*

'Cirrus' (photos this page)

# Dwarf Morning Glory
## Bush Morning Glory
*Convolvulus*

**Height:** 6–16" **Spread:** 10–12" **Flower color:** blue, purple, pink

THE WELL-MANNERED DWARF MORNING GLORY IS DELIGHTFUL. It has all the charm of a morning glory and does not share the invasive tendencies of its cousins, the bindweeds. I'm always willing to add blue and deep violet flowers to my garden, and several cultivars display true blue to deep blue violet hues. 'Royal Ensign' is a particular favorite. Its petals are edged with deep, true blue and the throat is sunny yellow surrounded by a white band. Dwarf morning glory is stunning combined with *Celosia argentea* 'Century Yellow' and *Heliotropium arborescens*.

## Planting

**Seeding:** Indoors in late winter; direct sow in mid- or late spring

**Planting out:** Mid- or late spring

**Spacing:** 8–12"

## Growing

Dwarf morning glory prefers **full sun.** The soil should be of **poor or average fertility** and **well drained.** This plant may not flower well in rich, moist soil.

Soak the seeds in water overnight before planting them. If starting seeds early indoors, plant them in peat pots to avoid root damage when transplanting.

*C. tricolor* (photos this page)

## Tips

Dwarf morning glory is a compact, mounding plant that can be grown on rock walls or in borders, containers or hanging baskets.

This easy-care plant is rarely plagued by pests or diseases.

## Recommended

*C. tricolor* bears flowers that last only a single day, blooming in the morning and twisting shut that evening. The species grows 12–16" tall. **Ensign Series** has low-growing, spreading plants growing 6" tall. **'Royal Ensign'** has deep blue flowers with white and yellow throats. **'Star of Yalta'** bears deep purple flowers that pale to violet in the throat.

*This annual is related to the bindweeds (*Convolvulus arvensis *and* C. sepium)*, but it doesn't share their unstoppable twining and spreading power.*

# Fan Flower

*Scaevola*

**Height:** up to 8" **Spread:** up to 36" or more **Flower color:** blue, purple

PLANTS INTRODUCED FROM AUSTRALIA HAVE CONSIDERABLY widened our choices for containers and seasonal displays. Fan flower's intriguing one-sided flowers add interest to a hanging basket or to the front of the garden. The flower color is difficult to pin down. It lies somewhere between blue and purple, and the quality of light—sun or shade—can affect our perception of its color. It shines in combination with white-flowered plants, which echo the spot of white at the base of fan flower's petals.

*Regular pinching and trimming will keep your fan flower bushy and blooming.*

## Planting

**Seeding:** Indoors in late winter

**Planting out:** After last frost

**Spacing:** 2–4'

## Growing

Fan flower grows well in **full sun** or **light shade**. The soil should be of **average fertility, moist** and very **well drained**. Water regularly because this plant doesn't like to dry out completely. It does, however, recover quickly from wilting when watered.

*S. aemula* cultivar

This attractive plant is actually a perennial that is treated as an annual. Cuttings can be taken during summer and new plants grown indoors to be used the following summer, or a plant can be brought in and kept in a bright room over winter. Seeds can be difficult to find.

## Tips

Fan flower is popular for hanging baskets and containers, but it can also be used along the tops of rock walls and in rock gardens where it can trail down. This plant makes an interesting addition to mixed borders or can be used under shrubs, where the long, trailing stems of fan flower will form an attractive groundcover.

## Recommended

*S. aemula* forms a mound of foliage from which trailing stems emerge. The fan-shaped flowers come in shades of purple, usually with white bases. The species is rarely grown because there are many improved cultivars. '**Blue Wonder**,' a Proven Winners cultivar, has long, trailing branches, making it ideal for hanging baskets. It can eventually spread 36" or more. 'Saphira' is a compact variety with deep blue flowers. It spreads about 12".

## Problems & Pests

Whiteflies may cause problems for fan flower if the plant becomes stressed from lack of water.

*Fan flower is native to Australia and Polynesia.*

*S. aemula* & *Impatiens hawkeri*

# Felicia
## Blue Marguerite, Blue Daisy
*Felicia*

**Height:** 10–24" **Spread:** 10–24" **Flower color:** many shades of blue or white; yellow centers

MY INTRODUCTION TO THE DIMINUTIVE-FLOWERED FELICIAS was in a topiary workshop. As part of the hands-on portion of the workshop, small shrubs were in flats ready to be trimmed and tied to the topiary form. A bonus was that the trimmings easily rooted, so I was able to propagate more plants. *Felicia amelloides* is actually a tender subshrub, and if you are patient you can grow it into a small topiary. Its cousin, *F. heterophylla,* is a true annual and does beautifully in containers as it surrounds the lower stems of taller plants.

## Planting

**Seeding:** Indoors in winter; direct sow in mid-summer

**Planting out:** After last frost

**Spacing:** 12"

*Felicias are sometimes called kingfisher daisies. The bright blue color of the flowers resembles the vivid hue of the European kingfisher's plumage.*

## Growing

Felicias like to grow in **full sun**. The soil should be of **average fertility** and **well drained**. These plants do not tolerate heat well and may fade when the weather heats up. Shear plants back to renew them or sow seed in mid-summer to provide flowers during cooler fall days.

Take cuttings from new fall growth of *F. amelloides* to start plants for the following spring. Taking cuttings will save you the uncertainty of starting with seeds or the trouble of trying to overwinter entire large plants.

## Tips

Felicias, with their sprawling habits, are well suited to rock gardens, bed edges, mixed containers and hanging baskets. The flowers close at night and on cloudy days.

The key to keeping these plants looking their best is trimming. When they are young, pinch the tips to promote bushiness. Deadhead as the flowers fade, and cut the plants back when the flowering slows down during the heat of summer. They will revive in the cooler fall weather and produce a second flush of growth and more flowers.

## Recommended

*F. amelloides* forms a rounded, bushy mound 12–24" in height and spread. It bears flowers of varied shades of blue all summer. This species is a perennial grown as an annual. '**Astrid Thomas**' is a dwarf variety with medium blue flowers. It grows 10" tall, with an equal spread. '**Midnight**' has deep blue flowers.

*F. heterophylla* forms a low mat of grayish green foliage. It bears blue, daisy-like flowers all summer and grows 10–24" tall, with an equal spread.

## Problems & Pests

Felicias are generally problem free, although aphids cause occasional trouble.

*F. amelloides* (photos this page)

# Flowering Flax

*Linum*

**Height:** 18–30"   **Spread:** 6"   **Flower color:** pink, white, red, blue, purple

THE WORD 'ELECTRIC' COMES TO MIND WHEN I SEE THE BLOOMS OF 'Rubrum' flowering flax. The intense red flowers with a hint of blue add a touch of excitement to the garden. These slender see-through plants are a perfect complement to boldly textured plants. Combine them with the true blue flowers of *Campanula medium* and the shimmering, silver dusty millers to create a pleasing composition. Increase the color by adding golden celosias and deep purple heliotropes.

*The related* L. usitatissimum *is the source of the flax seeds used to produce oil and linen fiber. It has been in cultivation for more than 7000 years.*

## Planting

**Seeding:** Direct sow in mid-spring

**Spacing:** 4–6"

## Growing

Flowering flax generally grows well in **full sun,** but during the heat of summer it enjoys protection from the hot afternoon sun, so it may be better off planted in partial shade. The soil should be of **average fertility, light, humus rich** and **well drained.**

'Caeruleum' (photos this page)

## Tips

Flowering flax can be used in borders and mixed containers and will nicely fill in the spaces between young perennials and shrubs in the landscape.

## Recommended

*L. grandiflorum* is an upright, branching plant. It grows 18–30" tall and spreads about 6". It bears dark-centered, light pink flowers. **'Bright Eyes'** bears white flowers with dark red or brown centers. It grows about 18" tall. **'Caeruleum'** bears blue or purple flowers. **'Rubrum'** bears deep red flowers on plants up to 18" tall.

## Problems & Pests

Excess moisture can cause trouble with stem rot and damping off. Slugs, snails and aphids can also cause problems.

*With its delicate appearance, flowering flax is a beautiful complement to plants with large, dramatic blooms.*

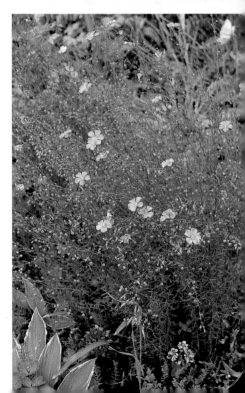

# Four-O'Clock Flower

*Mirabilis*

**Height:** 18–36" **Spread:** 18–24" **Flower color:** red, pink, magenta, yellow, white or bicolored

AN OLD-FASHIONED FAVORITE, FOUR-O'CLOCK FLOWER WAS frequently used in Victorian gardens and is often included in the heritage gardens of today. The name comes from the flowers' habit of opening at approximately four in the afternoon and remaining open through the next day. This makes them a perfect candidate for inclusion in a floral clock. The floral clocks of today have motorized hands that sweep across a face of plants. But historical floral clocks used plants that opened and closed at certain times of the day. What a perfect way to keep time and be in step with nature.

## Planting

**Seeding:** Indoors in late winter; direct sow in mid-spring

**Planting out:** Mid-spring

**Spacing:** 16–24"

## Growing

Four-o'clock flower prefers **full sun** but tolerates partial shade. The soil should be **fertile,** though any **well-drained** soil is tolerated. This plant grows well in moist soil, but it is heat and drought tolerant.

Four-o'clock flower is a perennial treated as an annual, and it may be grown from tuberous roots. Dig up the roots in fall, store them in a cool, dry place and replant them in spring to enjoy larger plants.

All parts of four-o'clock flower are poisonous, including the large black seeds. With the current trend of eating flowers, it is important that this plant be on the 'do not eat' list.

## Tips

Four-o'clock flower can be used in beds, borders, containers and window boxes. The flowers are scented, so the plant is often located near deck patios or terraces where the scent can be enjoyed in the afternoon and evening.

## Recommended

*M. jalapa* forms a bushy mound of foliage. The flowers may be solid or bicolored. A single plant may bear flowers of several colors. 'Marvel of Peru,' listed sometimes as a common name and sometimes as a cultivar, features the multi-colored flowers four-o'clock flower is known for. 'Red Glow' bears brilliant red flowers. 'Tea Time' bears a single flower color on each plant. Flowers may be red, white or pink.

## Problems & Pests

This plant has very few problems as long as it is given well-drained soil.

*Many species of moths are attracted to the fragrant flowers of this plant, which may bloom in several colors on a single plant.*

*M. jalapa* (photos this page)

# Fuchsia

*Fuchsia*

**Height:** 6–36" **Spread:** 6–36" **Flower color:** pink, orange, red, purple or white; often bicolored

'LUSCIOUS' IS THE WORD TO DESCRIBE THE BRIGHTLY COLORED flowers of the double fuchsias. Hummingbirds seem to agree, as fuchsias are among their favorite feeding stations. Fuchsias look great in the cool spring and fall, but they suffer in our extended periods of summer heat and humidity. There are two options: find a cool, shaded corner for them or plant one of the more heat-tolerant Triphylla hybrids. My current favorite is the scarlet, single-flowered 'Gartenmeister Bonstedt.' It is striking when combined with some of the silver-foliaged Rex begonias.

*Some gardeners who have kept fuchsias over several years have trained their plants to adopt a tree form.*

## Planting

**Seeding:** Not recommended

**Planting out:** After last frost

**Spacing:** 12–24"

## Growing

Fuchsias are grown in **partial** or **light shade**. They generally do not tolerate summer heat, and full sun can be too hot for them. The soil should be **fertile, moist** and **well drained**. Fuchsias need to be well watered, particularly in hot weather.

The plants can develop rot problems in soggy soil; ensure that the soil has good drainage. Fuchsias planted in well-aerated soil with plenty of perlite are almost impossible to overwater. As summer wears on, increase the amount of water given to container plants as the pots and baskets fill with thirsty roots. Fuchsias bloom on new growth, which will be stimulated by a high-nitrogen plant food.

Some fuchsias can be started from seed, although the germination rate can be poor and erratic. If you are up for the challenge, start the plants indoors in mid-winter. Ensure that the soil is warm, 68°–75° F. Seeds can take from two weeks to two months to sprout. It may be late summer, or even the following summer, before you see any floral reward for your efforts.

Although fuchsias are difficult to start from seed, they are easy to propagate from cuttings. Snip off 6" of new tip growth, remove the leaves from the lower third of the stem and insert the cuttings into soft soil or perlite. Once rooted and potted, the plants will bloom all summer.

'Winston Churchill' (above)

'Deep Purple'

'Gartenmeister Bonstedt'

Fuchsias are perennials that are grown as annuals. To store them over winter, cut back the plants to 6" stumps after the first light frost and place them in a dark, cold, but not freezing, location. Water just enough to keep the soil barely moist and do not feed. In mid-spring, repot the naked stumps, set them near a bright window and fertilize them lightly. Set your overwintered plants outdoors after all danger of frost has passed.

## Recommended

*Fuchsia* **hybrids** include hundreds of cultivars; just a few examples are given here. The upright fuchsias grow 18–36" tall, and the pendulous fuchsias grow 6–24" tall. Many of the available hybrids cannot be started from seed. '**Deep Purple**' has purple petals and white sepals. '**Florabelle**' is a good choice for starting from seed as the plants grow quickly to flowering size. The flowers are red and purple. The Triphylla hybrid '**Gartenmeister Bonstedt**' is an upright, shrubby cultivar that grows about 24" tall and bears tubular, orange-red flowers. The foliage is bronzy red with purple undersides. '**Snowburner**' has white petals and pink sepals. '**Swingtime**' has white petals with pink bases and pink sepals. This plant grows 12–24" tall, spreads about 6" and can be grown in a hanging basket or as a relaxed upright plant in beds and borders. '**Winston Churchill**' has purple petals and pink sepals. It grows 8–30" tall, with an equal spread. It is quite upright in form but is often grown in hanging baskets.

## Tips

Upright fuchsias can be used in mixed planters, beds and borders. The pendulous fuchsias are most often used in hanging baskets, but these flowers dangling from flexible branches also make attractive additions to planters and rock gardens.

Fuchsias should be deadheaded. Pluck the swollen seedpods from behind the fading petals or the seeds will ripen, robbing the plant of energy needed to produce flowers.

## Problems & Pests

Aphids, spider mites and whiteflies are common insect pests. Diseases such as crown rot, root rot and rust can be avoided with good air circulation and drainage.

*Children, and some adults, enjoy popping the fat buds of fuchsias. The temptation to squeeze them is almost irresistible.*

'Snowburner'

# Gazania

*Gazania*

**Height:** usually 6–8"; may reach 12–18" **Spread:** 8–12" **Flower color:** red, orange, yellow, pink, cream

HERE IS ANOTHER FABULOUS DAISY FROM SOUTH AFRICA. LIKE ITS cousins, gazania prefers to be in sunny sites as it tends not to bloom in low-light conditions, including cloudy days. And while the undersides of the petals are interesting, I prefer to see the inside of the flower. The Daybreak Series creates a colorful carpet under the summer-blooming star-of-Persia *(Allium christophii)*. This combination is a good match as both plants prefer sunny, drier spots in the garden.

*This native of southern Africa has very few pests and transplants easily, even when blooming.*

## Planting

**Seeding:** Indoors in late winter; direct sow after last frost

**Planting out:** After last frost

**Spacing:** 6–10"

## Growing

Gazania grows best in **full sun** but tolerates some shade. The soil should be of **poor to average fertility, sandy** and **well drained.** Gazania grows best in weather over 80° F and is drought tolerant.

Daybreak Series

## Tips

Low-growing gazania makes an excellent groundcover and is also useful on exposed slopes, in mixed containers and as an edging in flowerbeds. It is a wonderful plant for a xeriscape or dry garden design.

## Recommended

*G. rigens* forms a low basal rosette of lobed foliage. Large, daisy-like flowers with pointed petals are borne on strong stems above the plant. The petals often have a contrasting stripe or spot. The flowers tend to close on gloomy days and in low light. The species is rarely grown, but there are several hybrid cultivars available. **Daybreak Series** bears flowers in many colors, often with a contrasting stripe down the center of each petal. These flowers will stay open on dull days but close on rainy or very dark days. **Kiss Series** has compact plants that bear large flowers in several colors. Seeds are available by individual flower color or as a mix. **Mini-Star Series** has compact plants and flowers in many colors with a

contrasting dot at the base of each petal. **'Sundance'** bears flowers in reds and yellows with dark, contrasting stripes down the centers of the petals.

## Problems & Pests

Overwatering is the likely cause of any problems encountered by gazania.

*G. rigens* cultivars

# Geranium
## Pelargonium
### *Pelargonium*

**Height:** 8"–3'  **Spread:** 6"–4'  **Flower color:** red, pink, violet, orange, salmon, white, purple

PLANTS IN THE GENUS *PELARGONIUM* HAVE BEEN CALLED geraniums or annual geraniums for years because at one time they were included in the *Geranium* genus. Fortunately, this confusion about their identity hasn't affected their popularity. If you love flowing forms and abundant flowers, the ivy-leaved geraniums create beautiful hanging baskets or tender groundcovers. However, if you are looking for something out of the ordinary, seek out scented *Pelargonium* species for a visual and olfactory treat. My favorite, 'Peppermint,' has large, furry, maple-shaped leaves that release the scent of peppermint on warm days.

## Planting

**Seeding:** Indoors in early winter

**Planting out:** After last frost

**Spacing:** zonal geranium, about 12";
ivy-leaved geranium, 24–36";
scented geraniums, 12–36"

## Growing

Geraniums prefer **full sun** but tolerate partial shade, although they may
not bloom as profusely. The soil
should be **fertile** and **well drained**.

Geraniums are slow to grow from
seed, so purchasing plants may
prove easier. However, if you would
like to try starting your own from
seed, start them indoors in early
winter and cover them with clear
plastic to maintain humidity until
they germinate. Once the seedlings
have three or four leaves, transplant
them into individual 3–4" pots. Keep
your transplants in bright locations
because they need lots of light to
maintain their compact shape.

Deadheading is essential to keep
geraniums blooming and looking
neat. The flowerheads are attached
to long stems that break off easily
where they attach to the plant. Some
gardeners prefer to snip off just the
flowering end in order to avoid
potentially damaging the plant's
stem.

## Tips

Geraniums are very popular. Use
zonal geranium in beds, borders and
containers. Ivy-leaved geranium is
mostly used in hanging baskets and
containers but is also used as a bedding plant to form a bushy, spreading groundcover.

'Peppermint' (above)

Scented cultivar (center), *P. peltatum* (below)

*P. zonale* cultivar

Geraniums are tender perennials from South Africa that are treated as annuals. They can be kept indoors over winter in a bright room.

## Recommended

*P. peltatum* (ivy-leaved geranium) grows up to 12" tall and up to 4' wide. Many colors are available. Plants in the **Summer Showers Series** can take four or more months to flower from seed. **Tornado Series** is very good for hanging baskets and containers. The plants are quite compact, and the flowers are either lilac or white.

*P. zonale* (zonal geranium) grows up to 24" tall and 12" wide. Dwarf varieties grow up to 8" tall and 6" wide. The flowers are red, pink, purple, orange or white. Many of the zonal geraniums have contrasting bands of colors on their leaves. These often have to be propagated by cuttings to retain those characteristics. **Orbit Series** has attractive, compact, early-blooming plants. The seed is often sold in a mixed packet, but some individual colors are available. **Pillar Series** includes upright plants that grow up to 36" tall with staking. Salmon, violet and orange flowers are available. **Pinto Series** has flowers in all colors, and seed is generally sold by the color so you don't have to purchase a mixed packet and hope you like the colors you get. Flowers in the **Ripple Series** are speckled with darker and lighter shades of the main color. '**Raspberry Ripple**' bears salmon pink flowers speckled with white and red streaks.

*P.* **species and cultivars** (scented geraniums, scented pelargoniums) is a large group of geraniums that have scented leaves. The scents are grouped into the categories of rose, mint, citrus, fruit, spice and pungent. In the following list, a parent of each cultivar is indicated in parentheses. Some cultivars, such as '**Apple**' (*P. odoratissimum*), readily self-seed and stay true to form, but most must be propagated by cuttings to retain their ornamental and fragrant qualities. Many cultivars have variegated leaves. Intensely scented cultivars include '**Chocolate-Mint**' (*P. quercifolium*), '**Lemon**' (*P. crispum*), '**Nutmeg**' (*P.* x *fragrans*), '**Old-fashioned Rose**' (*P. graveolens*), '**Peppermint**' (*P. tomentosum*), '**Prince Rupert**' (*P. crispum*), '**Rober's Lemon Rose**' (*P. graveolens*) and '**Strawberry**' (*P.* x *scarboroviae*).

## Problems & Pests

Aphids will flock to overfertilized plants, but they can usually be washed off before they do much damage. Leaf spot and blight may bother geraniums growing in cool, moist soil.

Edema is an unusual condition to which geraniums are susceptible. This disease occurs when a plant is overwatered and absorbs so much of the water that the leaf cells burst. A warty surface develops on the leaves. It is more of a cosmetic problem as plants seem to continue to grow as long as the roots don't rot. There is no cure, although it can be avoided by watering carefully and removing any damaged leaves as the plant grows. The condition is more common in ivy-leaved geranium.

*Ivy-leaved geranium is one of the most beautiful plants to include in a mixed hanging basket.*

*P. zonale* cultivar (above), *P. peltatum* (below)

# Globe Amaranth

*Gomphrena*

**Height:** 6–30"  **Spread:** 6–15"  **Flower color:** purple, orange, magenta, pink, white, sometimes red

MY FIRST INTRODUCTION TO GLOBE AMARANTH WAS AT AN HERB society meeting. A member provided a gorgeous arrangement made from dried herbs and flowers for the refreshment table. These little flowers caught my eye. I inquired as to what they were and I was told that they were easy to grow, almost like weeds. So globe amaranth not only graced my garden the next season, it also became one of my favorite flowers to grow and to use. 'Strawberry Fields' is aptly named, with its intense orange-strawberry flowers. I have used it in the garden as a color punctuation point and in the vase as part of an autumn arrangement.

*Globe amaranth flowers are popular for cutting and drying because they keep their color and form well when dried. Harvest the blooms when they become round and plump, before the tiny flowers emerge, and dry them upside down in a cool, dry location.*

## Planting

**Seeding:** Indoors in late winter

**Planting out:** After last frost

**Spacing:** 10"

## Growing

Globe amaranth prefers **full sun.** The soil should be of **average fertility** and **well drained.** This plant likes hot weather. It needs watering only when drought-like conditions persist. Seeds will germinate more quickly if soaked in water for two to four days before sowing. They need warm soil, above 70° F, to sprout.

The long-lasting flowers require only occasional deadheading.

*G. globosa* (photos this page)

## Tips

Use globe amaranth in an informal or cottage garden. This plant is often underused because it doesn't start flowering until later in summer than many other annuals. Don't overlook it—the blooms are worth the wait, and they provide color from mid-summer until the first frost.

## Recommended

*G. globosa* forms a rounded, bushy plant 12–24" tall that is dotted with papery, clover-like flowers in purple, magenta, white or pink. **'Buddy'** is a more compact plant, 6–12" tall, with deep purple flowers. **'Lavender Lady'** grows into a large plant, up to 24" tall, and bears lavender purple flowers.

*G.* **'Strawberry Fields'** is a hybrid with bright orange-red or red flowers. It grows about 30" tall and spreads about half as much.

## Problems & Pests

Globe amaranth is susceptible to some fungal diseases, such as gray mold and leaf spot.

# Godetia
## Clarkia, Satin Flower
*Clarkia (Godetia)*

**Height:** 8"–4' **Spread:** 10–12" **Flower color:** pink, red, purple, white, some bicolored

GODETIA IS A BEAUTIFUL TRUE ANNUAL THAT DISLIKES OUR HOT summers. It is a West Coast native that grows on the edges of the coastal forests where cool breezes come in from the ocean. Not surprisingly, it is not particularly happy in hot, muggy Ohio. But, if you can find a relatively cool location that enjoys morning and noon sun, you might have a lovely plant in the fall when coolness returns.

### Planting

**Seeding:** Direct sow in spring for summer bloom or in mid- to late summer for fall flowers

**Spacing:** 6"

## Growing

Godetias grow equally well in **full sun** or **light shade**. The soil should be **well drained, light, sandy** and of **poor or average fertility**. Fertilizer will promote leaf growth at the expense of flower production. These plants don't like to be overwatered, so water sparingly and be sure to let them dry out between waterings. They do best in the cool weather of spring and fall.

Starting seeds indoors is not recommended. Seed plants where you want them to grow because they are difficult to transplant. Thin seedlings to about 6" apart.

## Tips

Godetias are useful in beds, borders, containers and rock gardens. The flowers can be used in fresh arrangements. These plants flower quickly from seed and can be planted in early spring to provide a show of satiny flowers before the hardier summer annuals steal the show. A planting in mid- to late summer will provide flowers in fall.

## Recommended

*C. amoena (Godetia amoena, G. grandiflora;* godetia, satin flower, farewell-to-spring) is a bushy, upright plant. It grows up to 30" tall, spreads 12" and bears clusters of ruffled, cup-shaped flowers in shades of pink, red, white and purple. **Satin Series** has compact plants that grow 8–12" tall. The single flowers come in many colors, including some bicolors.

*C. unguiculata (C. elegans;* clarkia, Rocky Mountain garland flower) is a

tall, branching plant that grows 1–4' high and spreads up to 10". Its small, ruffled flowers can be pink, purple, red or white. '**Apple Blossom**' bears apricot pink double flowers. '**Royal Bouquet**' bears very ruffled double flowers in pink, red or light purple.

## Problems & Pests

Root rot can occur if the soil is poorly drained.

*C. amoena* (photos this page)

# Heliotrope
## Cherry Pie Plant
*Heliotropium*

**Height:** 8"–4'  **Spread:** 12–24"  **Flower color:** purple, blue, white

HELIOTROPE HAS A SCENT THAT MOST PEOPLE LIKE, BUT IT IS difficult to describe. To me it smells like sweet baby powder, and I'll never understand how anyone could say it smells like a cherry pie. In addition to its scent, heliotrope offers beautiful flowers that attract many butterflies. The individual flowers are grouped so they provide a platform where a butterfly can sit and sip. At the herb garden at Inniswood Metro Gardens, a heliotrope standard adorns the fragrance garden where it attracts people and butterflies alike.

## Planting

**Seeding:** Indoors in mid-winter

**Planting out:** Once soil has warmed

**Spacing:** 12–18"

## Growing

Heliotrope grows best in **full sun.** The soil should be **fertile,** rich in **organic matter, moist** and **well drained.** Although overwatering will kill heliotrope, if left to dry to the point of wilting, the plant will be slow to recover.

Heliotrope is sensitive to cold weather, so plant it out after all danger of frost has passed. Protect plants with newspaper or a floating row cover (available at garden centers) if an unexpected late frost or cold snap should arrive. Container-grown plants can be brought indoors at night if frost is expected.

*H. arborescens* (all photos)

*This old-fashioned flower may have been popular in your grandmother's day. Its recent return to popularity comes as no surprise considering its attractive foliage, flowers and scent.*

## Tips

Heliotrope is ideal for growing in containers or beds near windows and patios where the wonderful scent of the flowers can be enjoyed.

This plant can be pinched and shaped. Create a tree form, or standard, by pinching off the lower branches as the plant grows until it reaches the height you desire; then pinch the top to encourage the plant to bush out. A shorter, bushy form is also popular and can be created by pinching all the tips that develop to encourage the plant to bush out at ground level.

Heliotrope can be grown indoors as a houseplant in a sunny window. A plant may survive for years if kept outdoors all summer and indoors all winter in a cool, bright room.

## Recommended

*H. arborescens* is a low, bushy shrub that is treated as an annual. It grows 18–24" tall, with an equal spread. Large clusters of purple, blue or white, scented flowers are produced all summer. Some new cultivars are not as strongly scented as the species. **'Blue Wonder,'** however, is a compact plant that was developed for heavily scented flowers. Plants grow up to 16" tall with dark purple flowers. **'Dwarf Marine'** ('Mini Marine') is a compact, bushy plant with fragrant, purple flowers. It grows 8–12" tall and also makes a good houseplant for a bright location. **'Fragrant Delight'** is an older cultivar with royal purple, intensely

fragrant flowers. It can reach a
height of 4' if grown as a standard.
'**Marine**' has violet blue flowers and
grows about 18" tall.

## Problems & Pests

Aphids and whiteflies can be
problems.

*Plants that are a little
underwatered tend to have
a stronger scent.*

# Hyacinth Bean
## Egyptian Bean, Lablab Bean
*Lablab (Dolichos)*

---

**Height:** 10–15'  **Spread:** variable  **Flower color:** purple, white; also grown for purple pods

WITH HYACINTH BEAN PLANTS AND SIX to eight 6' bamboo poles, you can create the perfect hiding place for a child. The resulting living teepee not only brings a smile to a child's face, it also creates a vertical garden accent that we adults can enjoy. Ensure that no one ever eats the poisonous raw beans. Typically we use hyacinth bean to climb trellises and walls, but another intriguing application is to let it roam on the ground through the feet of other plants. Imagine tall flowering *Nicotiana sylvestris* surrounded by the creeping stems of hyacinth bean.

## Planting

**Seeding:** Direct sow around last frost date, or start indoors in peat pots in early spring

**Planting out:** After last frost

**Spacing:** 12–18"

## Growing

Hyacinth bean prefers **full sun**. The soil should be **fertile, moist** and **well drained**.

## Tips

Hyacinth bean needs a trellis, net, pole or other structure to twine up. Plant it against a fence or near a balcony. If you grow it as a groundcover, make sure it doesn't engulf smaller plants.

## Recommended

*L. purpureus (Dolichos lablab)* is a vigorous twining vine. It can grow up to 30' tall, but when grown as an annual it grows about 10–15' tall. It bears many purple or white flowers over the summer, followed by deep purple pods.

## Problems & Pests

Rare problems with leaf spot can occur.

*The raw beans contain a cyanide-releasing chemical, so never eat the beans unless they are thoroughly cooked. The purple pods are edible if thoroughly cooked with two to four changes of water.*

# Impatiens
## Busy Lizzie, Touch-me-not
*Impatiens*

**Height:** 6–36" **Spread:** 12–24" **Flower color:** shades of purple, red, burgundy, pink, yellow, orange, apricot, white; also bicolored

I USED TO CONSIDER IMPATIENS BENEATH MY NOTICE because they were so common; then I was entranced by the hummingbirds that constantly visited a friend's hanging basket of impatiens. I was treated to the best example of territorial wars I had ever seen, proof that hummingbirds consider impatiens a choice selection. Hang a basket of the more brightly colored cultivars to initially attract the hummers. They will soon find any plants that you have placed at ground level. Then sit back and you will be treated to wonderful aerial displays. Recent introductions have widened the color range of the flowers, and many of the New Guinea cultivars have striking variegated foliage.

## Planting

**Seeding:** Indoors in mid-winter; balsam impatiens indoors in late winter

**Planting out:** Once soil has warmed

**Spacing:** 12–18"

## Growing

All impatiens do best in **partial shade** or **light shade** but tolerate full shade or, if kept moist, full sun. Of the various impatiens, New Guinea impatiens and balsam impatiens are the best adapted to sunny locations. The soil should be **fertile, humus rich, moist** and **well drained**. Though it is a heavy feeder, New Guinea impatiens does not like wet feet, so good drainage is a must.

Don't cover the seeds—they germinate best when exposed to light.

## Tips

Busy Lizzie is known for its ability to grow and flower profusely even in deep shade. Mass plant it in beds under trees, along shady fences or walls or in porch planters. It also looks lovely in hanging baskets. The new double-flowering varieties work beautifully as accent plants in hosta and wildflower gardens.

New Guinea impatiens is almost shrubby in form and is popular in patio planters, beds and borders. It grows well in full sun and may not flower as profusely in deep shade. This plant is grown as much for its variegated leaves as for its flowers.

Balsam impatiens was popular in the Victorian era and has recently experienced a comeback in popularity.

*I. balsamina* (above), *I. walleriana* (below)

*I. hawkeri* (photos this page)

This plant is more upright than the other two impatiens and is attractive when grouped in beds and borders.

## Recommended

New impatiens varieties are introduced every year, expanding the selection of sizes, forms and colors. The following list includes varieties that are popular year after year.

*I. balsamina* (balsam impatiens) grows 12–36" tall and up to 18" wide. The flowers come in shades of purple, red, pink or white. There are several double-flowered cultivars, such as '**Camellia-flowered**,' with pink, red or white flowers on plants up to 24" tall; '**Tom Thumb**,' with pink, red, purple or white flowers on plants to 12" tall; and '**Topknot**,' with large flowers in a similar range of colors held above the foliage on plants 12" tall.

*I. hawkeri* (New Guinea hybrids; New Guinea impatiens) grows 12–24" tall and 12" wide or wider. The flowers come in shades of red, orange, pink, purple or white. The foliage is often variegated with a yellow stripe down the center of each leaf. '**Java**' has bronzed leaves and flowers in lavender, salmon, pink or white. This cultivar can be grown from seed. '**Tango**' can also be grown from seed. This compact plant grows 12–18" tall and wide and has orange flowers.

*I.* '**Seashell**' is a new group of African hybrids with flowers in shades of yellow, orange, apricot and pink. Plants grow 8–10" tall and spread about 12".

*I. walleriana* (busy Lizzie) grows 6–18" tall and up to 24" wide. The flowers come in shades of red, orange, pink, purple or white, or are bicolored. **Elfin Series** is a common group of cultivars. The flowers are available in many shades, including bicolors. The compact plants grow about 12" tall, but they may spread more. **Fiesta Series** plants grow about 12" tall, with an equal spread, and bear double flowers in shades of pink, orange, red and burgundy. With their habit and flower form, they resemble small rose bushes. **Mosaic Series** has uniquely colored flowers, with the margins and most of the petals speckled in a darker shade of the petal color. **Tempo Series** has a wide range of colors, including bicolors, and flowers with contrasting margins on the petals. 'Victoria Rose' is an award-winning cultivar, with deep pink, double or semi-double flowers.

## Problems & Pests

Fungal leaf spot, stem rot, *Verticillium* wilt, whiteflies and aphids can cause trouble.

*I. walleriana* (photos this page)

*Impatiens come in a wide variety of heights, so be sure to check the tags before buying.*

# Lantana
## Shrub Verbena
*Lantana*

**Height:** 18–24"  **Spread:** up to 4'  **Flower color:** yellow, orange, pink, purple, red, white; often in combination

NATIVE TO THE TROPICAL REGIONS OF THE AMERICAS, LANTANA loves the heat of summer. It flowers best when sited in full sun, which is also the best location for attracting butterflies. Even though lantana is from far-away lands, our native butterflies thrive on its nectar. For a beautiful butterfly-attracting garden, combine the cultivar 'New Gold' with *Heliotropium arborescens* 'Dwarf Marine' and *Zinnia* 'Profusion White.' Lantanas can easily be trained into topiary. If you go to all that trouble or expense, make sure you have a cool porch where you can overwinter your plant.
Do not let your lantana freeze; it does not tolerate temperatures under 32° F.

## Planting

**Seeding:** Start seed indoors in spring; soil temperature 61°–64° F

**Planting out:** Into warm soil after danger of frost has passed

**Spacing:** 2–4'

## Growing

Lantana grows best in **full sun** but tolerates partial shade. The soil should be **fertile, moist** and **well drained,** but the plant can handle heat and drought.

If you would like to start plants for the following summer but don't want to store a large one over winter, take cuttings in late summer.

## Tips

Lantana is a tender shrub that is grown as an annual. It is useful in beds and borders as well as in mixed containers and hanging baskets.

## Recommended

*L. camara* is a bushy plant that bears round clusters of flowers in many colors. **'Feston Rose'** has flowers that open yellow and mature to bright pink. **'New Gold'** bears clusters of bright yellow flowers. **'Radiation'** has flowers that open yellow and mature to red.

*The flowers of lantana often open one color and mature to a completely different color, creating a striking display as several colors may appear in a single cluster at once.*

'Radiation'

*Lantana is rarely troubled by any pests or diseases and can handle hot weather, making it perfect for low-maintenance gardens.*

*L. camara* cultivar

# Larkspur

## Rocket Larkspur, Annual Delphinium
### *Consolida (Delphinium)*

**Height:** 1–4'  **Spread:** 6–14"  **Flower color:** blue, purple, pink, white

LARKSPUR IS THE PERFECT PASS-ALONG PLANT. IT IS EASY TO SHARE seeds and seedlings. I started with a handful of seeds six years ago, and I have had larkspur in my garden ever since. My stand, measuring 3' by 7', is a mixture of blue shades dotted with pale pink- and white-flowered plants. I've tried segregating the different colors, but somehow there is always this combination of soft pastels. It is a favorite early morning weeding area because being among those colors is a gentle way to start the day.

## Planting

**Seeding:** Indoors in mid-winter; direct sow in early or mid-spring, as soon as soil can be worked

**Planting out:** Mid-spring

**Spacing:** 12"

## Growing

Larkspur does equally well in **full sun** or **light shade**. The soil should be **fertile**, rich in **organic matter** and **well drained**. Keep the roots cool and add a light mulch; dried grass clippings or shredded leaves work well. Don't put mulch too close to the base of the plant, or crown rot may develop. Another option is to plant larkspurs close together so that the centers of plants are only 6–8" apart. Then the upper portion of the plants will shade the roots, so you will not need to use mulch.

Plant seeds in peat pots to prevent roots from being damaged when the plants are transplanted. Seeds started indoors may benefit from being chilled in the refrigerator for one week prior to sowing. Mix seeds in a plastic bag with moist peat moss or sand before placing them in the refrigerator.

Deadhead to keep larkspur blooming well into fall. Larkspur will self-sow, giving you more of these lovely plants to share.

## Tips

Plant groups of larkspur in mixed borders or cottage gardens. The tallest varieties may require staking to stay upright.

*C. ajacis*

## Recommended

*C. ajacis (C. ambigua, D. ajacis)* is an upright plant with feathery foliage. It bears spikes of purple, blue, pink or white flowers. **Dwarf Rocket Series** includes plants that grow 12–20" tall and 6–10" wide and bloom in many colors. **'Earl Grey'** grows 3–4' tall and bears flowers in an intriguing color between slate gray and gunmetal gray. **'Frosted Skies'** grows to 18" and bears large, semi-double flowers in a beautiful bicolor of blue and white. **Giant Imperial Series** has plants that grow 24–36" tall and up to 14" wide and come in many colors.

## Problems & Pests

Slugs and snails are potential problems. Powdery mildew and crown or root rot are avoidable if you water thoroughly, but not too often, and ensure good air circulation.

# Lavatera
## Mallow
*Lavatera*

**Height:** 20"–10'  **Spread:** 18"–5'  **Flower color:** pink, salmon, white, red, purple

IF YOU HAVE THE RIGHT SITE, LAVATERAS ARE SENSATIONAL. IN THE back of a garden bed they provide a bold textural backdrop. The catch is that they prefer a full sun location and cool nights. While we can provide the former, the latter is a bit unlikely in the middle of our hot, muggy Ohio summers. So, your lavatera may sulk, and possibly perish, in the heat of summer, but hopefully, it will revive in fall. Experiment with lavatera; search for that area where a breeze wafts through. You'll be glad you did.

*Though there are only 25 species of* Lavatera, *they are a diverse group comprising annuals, biennials, perennials and shrubs.*

## Planting

**Seeding:** Indoors in late winter; direct sow in spring

**Planting out:** After last frost

**Spacing:** 18–24"

## Growing

Lavatera prefers **full sun**. The soil should be of **average fertility, light** and **well drained**. These plants like cool, moist weather and may not flower much until the nights begin to cool in late summer. Select a site where the plants will be protected from strong winds.

These plants resent having their roots disturbed when they are transplanted and tend to do better when sown directly in the garden. If starting seeds indoors, use peat pots.

*L. cachemiriana* (photos this page), with *Verbena bonariensis* (below)

'Mont Blanc' (above), 'Silver Cup' (below)

## Tips

Lavatera plants can be used as colorful backdrops behind smaller plants in a bed or border. The blooms make attractive cut flowers and are edible.

Lavateras grow to be fairly large and shrubby. Stake tall varieties to keep them from falling over in summer rain showers.

## Recommended

*L. arborea* (tree mallow) is a large plant, capable of growing 10' tall and spreading 5'. The funnel-shaped flowers are pinkish purple. The life span of this plant is undetermined. Typically grown as an annual, it can sometimes be treated as a biennial or perennial. The cultivar **'Variegata'** has cream-mottled leaves.

*L. cachemiriana* has light pink flowers. It can grow up to 8' tall and is

usually half as wide. As the scientific name indicates, this plant is native to Kashmir.

*L. trimestris* is a bushy plant up to 4' tall and 18–24" in spread. It bears red, pink or white, funnel-shaped flowers. **Beauty Series** has plants in a variety of colors. '**Mont Blanc**' bears white flowers on compact plants that grow to about 20" tall. '**Silver Cup**' has cup-shaped light pink flowers with dark pink veins.

## Problems & Pests

Plant lavateras in well-drained soil to avoid root rot. Destroy any rust-infected plants.

*L. cachemiriana* (above), 'Mont Blanc' (below)

# Licorice Plant
## False Licorice
### *Helichrysum*

**Height:** 20" **Spread:** about 36"; sometimes up to 6' **Flower color:** yellow-white; plant grown for foliage

THE SILVERY SHEEN OF LICORICE PLANT IS CAUSED BY A FINE, SOFT pubescence on the leaves. This signals a preference for a sunny, drier location. Overwatering will cause your beautiful silver groundcover to change into a mushy mess. And please go easy on the fertilizer or your plant will become weak and floppy. So, actually, licorice plant is an easy-care tender perennial. It is a perfect complement to any plant, as silver is the ultimate blending color. A lovely combination is licorice plant with *Salvia farinacea* 'Victoria,' blue-eyed African daisy and the scented geranium *Pelargonium tomentosum* 'Peppermint.'

### Planting
**Seeding:** Not recommended

**Planting out:** After last frost

**Spacing:** About 30"

## Growing

Licorice plant prefers **full sun**. The soil should be of **poor to average fertility, neutral** or **alkaline** and **well drained**. Licorice plant wilts when the soil dries but revives quickly once watered. If it outgrows its space, snip it back with a pair of pruners.

Take cuttings in fall for a supply of new plants the next spring. Once they have rooted, keep the young plants in a cool, bright room for winter.

## Tips

Licorice plant is a perennial grown as an annual. It is prized for its foliage rather than its flowers. Include it in your hanging baskets and container plantings to provide a soft, silvery backdrop for the colorful flowers of other plants. Licorice plant can also be used as a groundcover or as an edger in beds and borders. It will cascade down in rock gardens and along the tops of retaining walls.

This is a good indicator plant for hanging baskets. When you see licorice plant wilting, it is time to water your baskets.

*H. petiolare* cultivar

## Recommended

*H. petiolare* is a trailing plant with fuzzy gray-green leaves. Cultivars are more common than the species. **'Limelight'** has bright lime green leaves that need protection from direct sun to maintain their color. **'Silver'** is a common cultivar with gray-green leaves covered in a silvery down. **'Silver Spike'** and **'Spike'** are newer, upright cultivars. A less common cultivar, **'Variegatum,'** has gray-green leaves dappled or margined in silvery cream.

## Problems & Pests

Powdery mildew can be an occasional problem.

'Silver' with *Verbena* & *Ricinus communis*

# Lisianthus
## Prairie Gentian
*Eustoma*

**Height:** 8–36"  **Spread:** usually half the height  **Flower color:** blue, purple, pink, yellow, white

LISIANTHUS IS LISTED AS AN ANNUAL, A BIENNIAL OR A SHORT-lived perennial native to the lower Central Plains and Mexico. Lisianthus may not know what it wants to be, but we like it anyway. The deeply colored, fragile petals have an ephemeral beauty and therefore are precious. This is one member of the gentian family that doesn't require acidic soil, but like its relatives, it requires good drainage. So, it is best to plant lisianthus in containers because our heavier clay soils are not favorable for its growth. This plant has become a favorite of the floral industry and is often sold as an ornamental potted plant much like cyclamen and poinsettias.

*A small vase filled with satin-textured lisianthus flowers will add a touch of elegance to any table.*

## Planting

**Seeding:** Indoors in early winter

**Planting out:** Mid-spring

**Spacing:** 4–12"

## Growing

Lisianthus prefers **full sun** but in hot weather benefits from light or partial shade providing protection from the afternoon sun. The soil should be of **average fertility** and **well drained**. A **neutral or alkaline soil** is preferred. If your soil is very acidic, grow the dwarf varieties in pots with an appropriate growing mix instead of struggling to keep lisianthus healthy in the garden beds.

Seedlings can be quite slow to establish when seeds are sown directly in the garden. It is best to either start lisianthus very early indoors with good light or purchase it at the garden center.

## Tips

All varieties of lisianthus look best grouped in flowerbeds or containers. The tallest varieties, with their long-lasting blooms, are popular in cut-flower gardens.

## Recommended

*E. grandiflorum* forms a slender, upright plant 24–36" tall topped by satiny, cup-shaped flowers. **Echo Series** is popular, with flowers in many colors. The plants are tall, to about 24", and are admired for their double flowers that are perfect for fresh arrangements. **Lisa Series** also comes in many colors. This popular dwarf variety, which grows to about 8" tall, is reputed to bloom from

seed one month sooner than other varieties.

## Problems & Pests

Generally, lisianthus is trouble free; however, several diseases, including *Fusarium* wilt, can kill it. Purchase treated seed from a reputable source, and destroy any afflicted plants before the diseases have a chance to spread.

*E. grandiflorum* (photos this page)

# Livingstone Daisy
## Ice Plant
*Dorotheanthus (Mesembryanthemum)*

**Height:** 6"  **Spread:** 12"  **Flower color:** pink, white, purple, crimson, orange, yellow or bicolored

LIVINGSTONE DAISY IS AN ANNUAL FROM SOUTH AFRICA, WHERE it grows in sandy soils of low fertility. It is a succulent that loves the heat but does not open its blooms on overcast days. This could be a problem in Ohio, which is known for having partly cloudy days throughout the growing season. Consider growing Livingstone daisy in those hot, dry corners where hens and chicks (*Sempervivum* spp.) survive so well.

## Planting

**Seeding:** Indoors in late winter; direct sow in spring

**Planting out:** After last frost

**Spacing:** 12"

## Growing

Livingstone daisy likes **full sun.** The soil should be of **poor to average fertility, sandy** and **well drained.** Livingstone daisy is very drought tolerant.

## Tips

Brightly flowered and low growing, Livingstone daisy can be used along edges of borders, on dry slopes, in rock gardens or in mixed containers. It can also be used between the stones or around the edges of a paved patio.

The flowers close on cloudy days.

## Recommended

*D. bellidiformis (M. criniflorum)* is a low-growing, spreading plant. It bears brightly colored, daisy-like flowers. Many of the cultivars may actually be hybrids between *D. bellidiformis* and *D. gramineus.* The compact plants of the **Gelato Series** bear many blooms. The brightly colored flowers usually have white or lighter-colored petal bases. **'Lunette'** ('Yellow Ice') bears bright yellow flowers with red centers. **Magic Carpet Series** plants have flowers in shades of purple, pink, white, yellow or orange. The petal bases are often lighter in color than the tips.

## Problems & Pests

Slugs, snails and aphids may be troublesome.

*D. bellidiformis* (above), 'Lunette' (below)

*The alternate common name, ice plant, refers to the fact that the leaves appear to glisten in the sun.*

# Lobelia
## Edging Lobelia
*Lobelia*

**Height:** 4–10" **Spread:** equal to height **Flower color:** purple, blue, pink, white, red

LOBELIA IS A COOL BLUE TRUE ANNUAL THAT BECOMES A SHRINKING violet when the hot weather hits in July and August. My neighbor is very conscientious about watering her plants during our mid-summer heat, and her lobelia never stops blooming, proof that a cooler location and some extra water helps lobelia bloom throughout the summer. One of my favorite combinations for the front of the garden is *Lobelia erinus* 'Crystal Palace' and *Alyssum maritima* 'Snow Crystal' planted at the feet of my perennial *Hosta* 'Inniswood.' The midnight blue lobelia intertwining with the sparkling white alyssum complements the chartreuse green of the hosta.

## Planting

**Seeding:** Indoors in mid-winter

**Planting out:** After last frost

**Spacing:** 6"

## Growing

Lobelia is often listed as a full sun annual, but it does better sited in **partial or light shade.** Avoid planting lobelia where it will be exposed to the late afternoon sun. The soil should be **fertile,** high in **organic matter, moist** and fairly **well drained.** Lobelia likes cool summer nights. In hot weather take care that its soil stays moist.

Lobelia seedlings are prone to damping off. See the section 'Starting Annuals from Seed' in the introduction for information on proper propagation techniques to help avoid damping off.

## Tips

Use lobelia along the edges of beds and borders, on rock walls, in rock gardens, in mixed containers or in hanging baskets.

Trim lobelia back after the first wave of flowers. It will stop blooming in the hottest part of summer but will revive in fall if you continue to water it regularly over the summer.

## Recommended

*L. erinus* may be rounded and bushy or low and trailing. It bears flowers in shades of blue, purple, red, pink or white. **Cascade Series** plants have a trailing form; flowers come in many shades. **'Crystal Palace'** is a compact plant that rarely grows over 4" in height. This cultivar has dark

green foliage and dark blue flowers. The cultivars in the **Regatta Series** are trailing; they tolerate heat better and bloom longer than other cultivars. **Riviera Series** has flowers in shades of blue and purple on bushy plants. **'Sapphire'** has white-centered blue flowers on trailing plants.

## Problems & Pests

Rust, leaf spot and slugs may be troublesome.

Cascade Series (above), 'Sapphire' (below)

# Love-in-a-Mist
## Devil-in-a-Bush
### *Nigella*

**Height:** 16–24 " **Spread:** 8–12 " **Flower color:** blue, white, pink, purple

LOVE-IN-A-MIST IS PROBABLY THE PLANT I SHARE MOST FROM MY garden. During a season, I can have up to three generations of plants, so there are always some plants in seed and some in bloom. It is difficult to decide which I like best. The baby blue flowers create a lovely backdrop for bulbs and perennials while the puffed seedpods add notes of tan and maroon to the garden. These traits spark questions such as 'Do you have any seed or plants to spare?' I am happy to share, and any unwanted seedlings go into the compost pile so they may enrich future generations.

*Both the flowers and the seedpods are popular for flower arrangements. The flowers are long lasting in fresh arrangements, and the pods can be dried when ripe and added to dried arrangements.*

## Planting

**Seeding:** Indoors in late winter; direct sow in early spring

**Planting out:** Mid-spring

**Spacing:** 10–15"

## Growing

Love-in-a-mist prefers **full sun.** The soil should be of **average fertility, light** and **well drained.**

Direct sow seeds at two-week intervals all spring to prolong the blooming period. This plant resents having its roots disturbed. Seeds started indoors should be planted in peat pots or pellets to avoid damaging the roots when the plant is transplanted into the garden.

Love-in-a-mist has a tendency to self-sow and may show up in unexpected spots in your garden for years to come. Its ferny foliage and delicate blue flowers blend with most plants.

## Tips

This attractive, airy plant is often used in mixed beds and borders. The flowers appear to float above the delicate foliage. The blooming may slow and the plants may die back if the weather gets too hot in summer.

The stems of this plant can be a bit floppy and may benefit from being staked with twiggy branches. Poke the branches in around the plants while they are young, and the plants will grow up between the twigs.

## Recommended

*N. damascena* forms a loose mound of finely divided foliage. It grows 18–24" tall and spreads about half

this much. The light blue flowers darken as they mature. Plants in the **Miss Jekyll Series** grow to about 18" high and bear semi-double flowers in rose pink, sky blue or a deep cornflower blue that pairs especially well with golden yellow coreopsis. **'Mulberry Rose'** bears light pink flowers that mature to dark pink. **Persian Jewel Series** contains some of the most common cultivars, with plants that usually grow to 16" tall and have flowers in many colors.

*N. damascena* (photos this page)

# Marigold

*Tagetes*

**Height:** 7–36" **Spread:** 12–24" **Flower color:** yellow, red, orange, brown, gold, cream, bicolored

WHEN I WAS YOUNG WE PLANTED MARIGOLDS EVERY YEAR. IN science class we placed these seeds into milk cartons to learn how tiny seeds become plants, and these magical plants became Mother's Day gifts. In the garden marigolds were the flowers we were allowed to plant ourselves. Marigolds are tough and are perfect for little hands to transplant. There is something about stepping back and seeing your row—albeit a bit uneven— that makes you proud. These memories have stayed in my heart for years. And, although marigolds are common, they are very special to me.

## Planting

**Seeding:** Start indoors in spring or earlier

**Planting out:** Once soil has warmed

**Spacing:** Dwarf marigolds, 6"; tall marigolds, 12"

## Growing

Marigolds grow best in **full sun**. The soil should be of **average fertility** and **well drained**. These plants are drought tolerant and hold up well in windy, rainy weather.

Remove spent blooms to encourage more flowers and to keep plants tidy.

## Tips

Mass planted or mixed with other plants, marigolds make a vibrant addition to beds, borders and container gardens. These plants will thrive in the hottest, driest parts of your garden.

*T. erecta* (above), *T. patula* with *Lobelia* (below)

*When using marigolds as cut flowers, remove the lower leaves to take away some of the pungent scent.*

T. tenuifolia (above), T. erecta (below)

*T. erecta and* T. patula *are often used in vegetable gardens for their reputed insect-repelling qualities.*

## Recommended

*T. erecta* (African marigold, American marigold, Aztec marigold) is 20–36" tall and bears huge flowers. **Cracker Jack Series** plants reach 36" in height and bear large double flowers in bright shades of orange and yellow. '**Inca**' bears double flowers in solid or multi-colored shades of yellow, gold and orange on compact plants that grow to 18" tall. '**Marvel**' is another compact cultivar, growing only 18" tall, but with the large flowers that make the species popular. '**Vanilla**' bears cream white flowers, a unique color for marigolds, on compact, odorless plants.

*T. patula* (French marigold) is low growing, only 7–10" tall. The double-flowered plants in the popular **Bonanza Series** are red, orange, yellow and bicolored. **Janie Series** is a popular group of double-flowered cultivars. The early-blooming, compact plants have red, orange and yellow blooms.

*T. tenuifolia* (Signet marigold) has dainty single flowers that grow on bushy plants with feathery foliage. **Gem Series** plants are commonly available. The compact plants, about 10" tall, bear flowers in shades of yellow ('**Yellow Gem**') and orange ('**Orange Gem**'), producing blooms all summer; the flowers are edible. '**Starfire**' bears single flowers in shades of yellow, orange and red, all with a band of dark red near the base of each petal.

*T.* **Triploid Hybrids** (triploid marigold) have been developed by crossing *T. erecta* and *T. patula*. The resulting plants have the huge flowers of African marigold and the compact growth of French marigold. These hybrids are the most heat resistant of all the marigolds. They grow about 12" tall and spread 12–24". 'Nugget' bears large yellow, red, orange, gold or bicolored flowers on low, wide-spreading plants.

## Problems & Pests

Slugs and snails can chew marigold seedlings to the ground.

T. tenuifolia *is used as a culinary or tea herb in some Latin American countries, and its petals add a piquant note to a salad.*

*T. patula* cultivar (above), *T. tenuifolia* (below)

# Mexican Sunflower

*Tithonia*

**Height:** 18"–6'  **Spread:** 12–24"  **Flower color:** orange, red-orange, yellow

WHETHER IT IS THE TALLER SPECIES OR THE DIMINUTIVE CULTIVAR 'Fiesta del Sol,' this plant elicits a comment from all who pass by. Mexican sunflower, like many other members of the daisy family, is a wonderful supporter of wildlife. In summer it is visited by myriad butterflies and insects. In fall it provides seed for birds. The taller species and cultivars of Mexican sunflower tend to delay blooming until mid-summer because they are spending their energy creating a massive shrub-like habit. 'Fiesta del Sol' has bloomed earlier for me. Combine with the perennial *Aster novae-angliae* 'Purple Dome' and little bluestem grass *(Schizachyrium scoparium)* for a beautiful fall vignette.

*For a hot look along a sunny fence or wall, mix Mexican sunflower with other sunflowers and marigolds.*

## Planting

**Seeding:** Indoors in early spring; direct sow in spring

**Planting out:** Once soil has warmed

**Spacing:** 12–24"

## Growing

Mexican sunflower grows best in **full sun**. The soil should be of **average to poor fertility** and **well drained**. Cover seeds lightly; they germinate more evenly and quickly when exposed to some light. Mexican sunflower needs little water or care; however, if deadheaded regularly, it will bloom more profusely and until the first moderate frost.

## Tips

Mexican sunflower is heat resistant, so it is ideal for growing in a sunny, dry, warm spot such as under the eaves of a south-facing wall. The plants are tall and break easily if exposed to too much wind; grow along a wall or fence to provide them shelter and stability. This annual has a coarse appearance and is well suited to the back of a border, where it will provide a good backdrop to a bed of shorter plants.

## Recommended

*T. rotundifolia* is a vigorous, bushy plant. It grows 3–6' tall and spreads 12–24". Vibrant orange-red flowers are produced from mid- to late summer through to frost. '**Fiesta del Sol,**' an All-America Selections winner, bears bright orange flowers on plants that grow 18–30" tall. '**Goldfinger**' grows 24–36" tall and bears large orange flowers. '**Torch**'

has red-orange flowers, and '**Yellow Torch**' has bright yellow flowers.

## Problems & Pests

This plant is resistant to most problems; however, young foliage may suffer slug and snail damage. Aphids can become a real problem if not dealt with immediately.

*T. rotundifolia* (above), 'Torch' (below)

# Million Bells
## Calibrachoa, Trailing Petunia
*Calibrachoa*

**Height:** 6–12" **Spread:** up to 24" **Flower color:** pink, purple, yellow, red-orange, white, blue

MILLION BELLS IS CHARMING, AND GIVEN THE RIGHT CONDITIONS, blooms continually during the growing season. A tender spreading shrub, million bells has performed better for me in a container, which speaks to its need for good drainage. Unfortunately, my attempt to overwinter it resulted in a sad, soggy mess. But I enjoy purchasing new plants in spring, as every year there are new selections to consider.

*Million bells has been found to be hardy in Zone 7, where it can grow into its shrub form.*

## Planting

**Seeding:** Seeds may not be available

**Planting out:** After last frost

**Spacing:** 6–15"

## Growing

Million bells plants prefer **full sun.** The soil should be **fertile, moist** and **well drained.** Though it prefers to be watered regularly, million bells is fairly drought resistant once established. It will bloom well into fall; the flowers become hardier over summer and as the weather cools.

## Tips

Popular for planters and hanging baskets, million bells is also attractive in beds and borders. It grows all summer and needs plenty of room to spread or it will overtake other flowers. Pinch back to keep plants compact. In a hanging basket, it will produce plentiful bell-shaped blooms.

To protect the petals from rain, place hanging baskets under the eaves of the house or porch.

## Recommended

*Calibrachoa* **hybrids** have a dense, trailing habit. They bear small flowers that look like petunias. **Million Bells Series** includes 'Cherry Pink,' with reddish pink flowers on upright plants; 'Terracotta,' with reddish orange flowers and an upright habit; 'Trailing Blue,' with dark blue or purple, yellow-centered flowers; 'Trailing Pink,' with rose pink, yellow-centered flowers; 'Trailing White,' with white, yellow-centered flowers; and 'Yellow,' with bright yellow flowers.

## Problems & Pests

Wet weather and cloudy days may cause leaf spot and delayed blooming. Slugs like to nibble on the petals.

'Trailing Pink' with *Petunia* (above), 'Terracotta' (below)

# Monkey Flower

*Mimulus*

**Height:** 6–12" **Spread:** 12–24" **Flower color:** bright and pastel shades of orange, yellow, burgundy, pink, red, cream or bicolors

MONKEY FLOWER BLOSSOMS LOOK LIKE COLORFUL CHIMPANZEE faces, especially if you squint your eyes a bit. The secret to successfully growing monkey flower in Ohio is finding a moist spot that is warm in the day and cool in the late afternoon and evening. An eastern exposure with cool evening breezes is perfect. I have to admit that I have been more successful finding these plants in the wild in Colorado than raising them in my hot, sunny garden. But hope springs eternal, and one of these days I may find or create that perfect spot.

## Planting

**Seeding:** Indoors in early spring

**Planting out:** Once soil warms after last frost

**Spacing:** 10–12"

## Growing

Monkey flowers prefer **partial or light shade**. Protection from the afternoon sun will prolong the blooming of these plants. The soil should be **fertile, evenly moist** and **humus rich**. Don't allow the soil to dry out. These plants can become scraggly and unattractive in hot sun.

'Mystic' (photos this page)

## Tips

Monkey flowers make an excellent addition to a border near a pond or to a bog garden. In a flowerbed, border or container garden, the plants will need to be watered regularly.

These plants are perennials grown as annuals. They can be overwintered indoors in a cool, bright room.

## Recommended

*M.* x *hybridus (M. guttatus* x *M. luteus)* is a group of upright plants with spotted flowers. They grow 6–12" tall and spread 12". **'Calypso'** bears a mixture of flower colors. **'Mystic'** is compact and early flowering and offers a wide range of bright flower colors in solids or bicolors.

*M. luteus* (yellow monkey flower), though not as commonly grown as *M.* x *hybridus*, is worth growing for its spreading habit and yellow flowers. It grows about 12" tall and spreads up to 24". The flowers are sometimes spotted with red or purple.

*The cheerful blooms of these plants bring to mind a monkey's face, hence the common name. In a similar vein, the genus name,* Mimulus, *means 'little actor' or 'little mime.'*

## Problems & Pests

Downy or powdery mildew, gray mold, whiteflies, spider mites and aphids can cause occasional problems.

# Morning Glory
## Moonflower, Sweet Potato Vine, Mina Lobata
### *Ipomoea*

**Height:** 6–15'  **Spread:** 1–15'  **Flower color:** white, blue, pink, red, yellow, orange, purple, sometimes bicolored

YOU HAVE TO BE CAREFUL WHEN INVITING SOME SPECIES AND cultivars of morning glories into the garden because several have a habit of overwhelming other plants. However, when you find an appropriate use and location, most are a delight. At our first home, 'Heavenly Blue' created a beautiful boundary out of an ugly chain-link fence. It contrasted well with the bishop's goutweed, a thug if ever there was one, which traveled over from our neighbor's yard. It would have been an interesting experiment to allow the morning glory to grow as a groundcover. I wonder which plant would have won...

## Planting

**Seeding:** Indoors in early spring; direct sow after last frost

**Planting out:** Late spring

**Spacing:** 12–18"

## Growing

Grow these plants in **full sun**. Any soil will do, but a **light, well-drained** medium of **poor to average fertility** is preferred. Moonflower *(I. alba)* needs warm weather to bloom.

These plants must twine around objects in order to climb them. Wide fence posts, walls or other broad objects must have a trellis or some wire or twine attached to them to provide the vines with something to grow on.

Soak seeds for 24 hours before sowing. If starting seeds indoors, sow them in individual peat pots.

*Grow moonflower on a trellis near a porch or patio that is used in the evenings, so that the sweetly scented flowers can be fully enjoyed. Once evening falls, the huge, white blossoms pour forth their sweet nectar, attracting night-flying moths.*

*I. purpurea* (above), *I. alba* (below)

*I. purpurea* (above), *I. batatas* 'Tricolor' (below)

## Tips

These vines can be grown on fences, walls, trees, trellises and arbors. As groundcovers, morning glories will grow over any obstacles they encounter. They can also be grown in hanging baskets.

If you have a bright sunny window, consider starting a hanging basket of morning glories indoors for a unique winter display. The vines will twine around the hangers and spill over the sides of the pot, providing you with beautiful trumpet flowers, regardless of the weather outside.

Each flower of a morning glory plant lasts one day. Each bud forms a spiral that slowly unfurls as the day brightens with the rising sun.

## Recommended

*I. alba* (moonflower) is a twining climber that has sweet-scented, white flowers that open only at night. It grows up to 15' tall.

*I. batatas* (sweet potato vine) is a twining climber that is grown for its attractive foliage rather than its flowers. Often used in planters and hanging baskets, it can be used by itself or mixed with other plants. It may spread or climb 10' or more in a summer. '**Blackie**' has dark purple (almost black), deeply lobed leaves. '**Marguerite**' ('Terrace Lime') has yellow-green foliage on fairly compact plants. This cascading plant can also be trained to grow up a trellis. '**Tricolor**' has green, white and pink variegated foliage. As a bonus, when you pull up your plant at the end of summer, you can eat any tubers (sweet potatoes) that have formed.

*I. lobata* (mina lobata, firecracker vine, exotic love) is a twining climber 6–15' tall. The flowers are borne along one side of a spike. The buds are red and the flowers mature to orange then yellow, giving the spike a fire-like appearance.

*I. purpurea* (common morning glory) is a twining climber that grows 6–10' tall. It bears trumpet-shaped flowers in purple, blue, pink or white. '**Grandpa Ott**' bears pinky purple flowers with darker purple stripes. '**Knowilan's Black**' bears dark purple flowers.

*I. tricolor* (morning glory) is a twining climber that grows 10–12' tall in one summer. Many cultivars of this species are available, although some listed as such may actually be cultivars of *I. nil* or *I. purpurea*. '**Blue Star**' bears blue-and-white-streaked flowers. '**Heavenly Blue**' bears sky blue flowers with white centers.

## Problems & Pests

Morning glories are susceptible to several fungal problems, but they occur only rarely.

'Blackie' with annuals (above), 'Marguerite' (below)

*Sweet potato vine is best recognized by its large, lime green, heart-shaped leaves, but the foliage is also available in shades of purple. Unlike the more aggressive morning glory species, sweet potato vine doesn't twine or grasp or get carried away. Instead, it drapes politely over the sides of containers or spreads neatly over the soil beneath taller plants.*

# Moss Rose
## Portulaca
*Portulaca*

**Height:** 4–8" **Spread:** 6–12" or more **Flower color:** red, pink, yellow, white, purple, orange, peach

IT IS DIFFICULT TO FIND A PLANT THAT WILL GROW AROUND THE mailbox next to an asphalt street. Most people would choose the orange daylily, which grows anywhere. My neighbor built a small raised bed and planted moss rose. It gracefully trailed over the small wall and provided color for most of the summer. It also self-seeded for a few years before disappearing. One of the downsides to moss rose has been its habit of staying closed on cloudy days. The 'Cloudbeater' cultivars have been selected for their ability to bloom even when the skies are gray. We especially appreciate their dainty beauty on an overcast day.

## Planting

**Seeding:** Indoors in late winter

**Planting out:** Once soil has warmed

**Spacing:** 12"

## Growing

Moss rose requires **full sun**. The soil should be of **poor fertility, sandy** and **well drained**. To ensure that you will have plants where you want them, start seed indoors. If you sow directly outdoors, the tiny seeds may get washed away by rain and the plants will pop up in unexpected places. Spacing the plants close together is not a problem; in fact, the intertwining of the plants and colorful flowers creates an interesting and attractive effect.

## Tips

Moss rose is the ideal plant for garden spots that just don't get enough water—under the eaves of the house or in dry, rocky, exposed areas. It is also ideal for people who like baskets hanging from the front porch but only occasionally remember to water them. As long as the location is sunny, this plant will do well with minimal care.

## Recommended

*P. grandiflora* forms a bushy mound of succulent foliage. It bears delicate, papery, rose-like flowers profusely all summer. '**Cloudbeater**' bears large double flowers in many colors. The flowers stay open all day, even in cloudy weather. '**Sundance**' plants are low spreading, with semi-double and double flowers in a wide range of colors. **Sundial Series** plants have

long-lasting double flowers. '**Sundial Peach**' is an All-America Selections winner; it has double flowers in shades of peach.

## Problems & Pests

If moss rose has excellent drainage and as much light as possible, it shouldn't have problems.

*Moss rose will fill a sunny, exposed, narrow strip of soil next to pavement with bright colors all summer. It requires only minimal attention.*

*P. grandiflora* (photos this page)

# Nasturtium

*Tropaeolum*

**Height:** 12–18" for dwarf varieties; up to 10' for trailing varieties
**Spread:** equal to or slightly greater than height  **Flower color:** red, orange, yellow, burgundy, pink, cream, gold, white or bicolored

NASTURTIUMS ARE A MAINSTAY ANNUAL IN MY GARDEN AND IN my kitchen. I use the flowers and leaves as garnishes, in salads and as pizza toppings. But beware of hiding insects—clean the flowers and leaves well. Earwigs love to nestle into the deep calyx of the nasturtium flower. It is unsettling to a dinner guest to see an earwig run out of the salad bowl as the dressing is added. And while black aphids may look like poppy seeds, they are not an acceptable substitute.

## Planting

**Seeding:** Indoors in late winter; direct sow around last frost date

**Planting out:** After last frost

**Spacing:** 12"

## Growing

Nasturtiums prefer **full sun** but tolerate some shade. The soil should be of **average to poor fertility, light, moist** and **well drained**. Too rich a soil or too much nitrogen fertilizer will result in lots of leaves and very few flowers. Let the soil drain completely between waterings.

If you start nasturtium seeds indoors, sow them in individual peat pots to avoid disturbing the roots during transplanting.

*Nasturtiums have a place in any vegetable or herb garden. The leaves and flowers are edible and can be added to salads, soups and dips. They have a peppery flavor, so don't overdo it. The unripe seedpods can be pickled and used as a substitute for capers (see p. 219).*

Alaska Series (above), *T. majus* and lettuce in kitchen garden (below)

*T. majus* (above), Alaska Series (below)

## Tips

Nasturtiums are used in beds, borders, containers and hanging baskets and on sloped banks. The climbing varieties are grown up trellises or over rock walls or places that need concealing. These plants thrive in poor locations, and they make an interesting addition to plantings on hard-to-mow slopes.

Some gardeners believe that nasturtiums attract and harbor certain pests, such as whiteflies and aphids, and that they should not be grown near plants that are susceptible to the same problems. Other gardeners believe that pest insects prefer nasturtiums and will flock to them and leave the rest of the garden alone. Still other gardeners claim that these plants, because of the high sulfur levels in the leaves, repel many pests that would otherwise infest the garden. If you do find aphids on the plants, you will notice that they congregate near the growing tips. Cut the infested parts off and drop them in a bucket of soapy water to rid your plants of this problem.

Don't assume that dwarf cultivars stay small. I planted one of the Jewel Series cultivars hoping for small, bushy plants and found they outstripped my scarlet runner beans in the race to the top of the fence. The range of flower colors was stunning, and I really didn't mind their rampant behavior.

## Recommended

*T. majus* has a trailing habit. It has been greatly improved by hybridizing. The foliage of the older varieties tended to hide the flowers, but new varieties hold their flowers (available in a great selection of colors) above the foliage. There are also some new and interesting cultivars with variegated foliage and compact, attractive, mound-forming habits. **Alaska Series** plants have white-marbled foliage. **Jewel Series** plants are compact, growing to 12" tall and wide, with double flowers in a mix of deep orange, red or gold. **'Peach Melba'** forms a 12" mound. The flowers are pale yellow with a bright orange-red splash at the base of each petal. **'Whirlybird'** is a compact, bushy plant. The single or double flowers in shades of red, pink, yellow or orange do not have spurs.

'Peach Melba' (above), Alaska Series (below)

*T. peregrinum* (canary bird vine, canary creeper) is a vigorous climber with five-lobed leaves. It grows about 10' tall. The yellow flowers are borne in loose clusters. The two upper petals of each flower are fringed, giving the flowers a bird-like appearance.

## Problems & Pests

The few problems that afflict nasturtiums include aphids, slugs, whiteflies and some viruses.

# RECIPE

### Poor Man's Capers (Pickled Nasturtium Seedpods)

Soak green seedpods for 24 hours in a brine made from 2 cups of water and 1 tbsp. salt.

Pack small, sterilized jars with the seedpods, one peeled clove of garlic and 1 tsp. pickling spices.

Heat white wine vinegar to simmering and fill each jar with the vinegar.

Seal with acid-proof lids and let the seedpods sit for about a month.

*The pickled seedpods should be eaten within a week after opening.*

# Nemesia

*Nemesia*

**Height:** 6–24"  **Spread:** 4–12"  **Flower color:** red, blue, purple, pink, white, yellow, orange or bicolored

THE RICH FLORA OF SOUTH AFRICA HAS BEEN THE ORIGIN OF many wonderful garden plants, many from areas that have abundant rainfall and moderate temperatures during the growing season. Nemesia is a tender perennial that enjoys these temperate conditions, which is why we sometimes have difficulty growing it in our hotter summers of little rain. The best way to grow nemesia is to plant mature plants in early spring, keep them moist and cool in the dog days of summer and then let them shine again in fall.

## Planting

**Seeding:** Start indoors in early spring

**Planting out:** After last frost

**Spacing:** 6"

## Growing

Nemesias prefer **full sun**. The soil should be **average to fertile, slightly acidic, moist** and **well drained**. Regular watering will keep these plants blooming through the summer.

## Tips

Nemesias make a bright and colorful addition to the front of a mixed border or mixed container planting.

## Recommended

*N. strumosa* is a perennial that is sometimes grown as an annual and forms a bushy mound of bright green foliage. It grows 6–24" tall and spreads 4–12". It bears flowers in shades of blue, purple, white, pink, red or yellow, often in bicolors. There are many cultivars attributed to this species, but some are probably of hybrid origin. **'Bluebird'** bears lavender blue flowers on plants 8–12" tall. **Carnival Series** plants are compact and bear many flowers in yellow, white, orange, pink or red. **'Compact Innocence'** bears white flowers. **'KLM'** has bicolored blue and white flowers with yellow throats. **'National Ensign'** ('Red and White') bears flowers bicolored red and white.

## Problems & Pests

Occasional problems with crown or root rot are possible.

'KLM' (above), 'National Ensign' (below)

*Combine the blue and white flowers of 'KLM' with the red and white of 'National Ensign,' and celebrate the Fourth of July all summer.*

# Nicotiana
## Flowering Tobacco Plant
*Nicotiana*

---

**Height:** 1–5'  **Spread:** 12"  **Flower color:** red, pink, purple, green, yellow, white

ONE OF MY GARDEN AMBITIONS IS TO CREATE THE PERFECT DUSK garden. The period between day and night has a luminous quality and some flowers take on a shimmering glow as the sun sets. *N. sylvestris* is one of those flowers. It has the added attraction of releasing a sweet, elusive perfume in the evening. I planted it by a bench in my garden about six years ago, and seedlings sprout every year, making that bench a favorite dusk destination.

## Planting

**Seeding:** Indoors in early spring; direct sow once soil warms

**Planting out:** Once soil has warmed

**Spacing:** 8–12"

## Growing

Nicotianas grow equally well in **full sun, light shade** or **partial shade.** The soil should be **fertile,** high in **organic matter, moist** and **well drained.**

The seeds require light for germination, so leave them uncovered.

## Tips

Nicotianas are popular in beds and borders. The dwarf varieties do well in containers. Do not plant nicotianas near tomatoes because, as members of the same plant family, they share a vulnerability to many of the same diseases. The nicotiana plant may attract and harbor diseases that will hardly affect it but that can kill tomatoes.

*N. sylvestris* (above), Nicki Series (below)

*Nicotianas were originally cultivated for the wonderful scent of the flowers. The first plants had green flowers that opened only in the evening and at night. In attempts to expand the variety of colors and the daily blooming period, the popular scent has sometimes been lost.*

N. *sylvestris* (photos this page)

## Recommended

N. *langsdorffii* grows up to 3–5' tall. It bears clusters of green flowers. The leaves and stems are hairy and feel sticky to the touch.

N. 'Lime Green' produces green, star-like flowers on upright plants that grow to 30" tall.

N. x *sanderae* (N. *alata* x N. *forgetiana*) is a hybrid that grows up to 5' tall. The parents are fragrant but the hybrid is lightly scented to scentless. Domino Series plants are compact, growing 12–18" tall with an equal spread. The flowers come in many colors and stay open all day. Merlin Series has dwarf plants ideal for mixed planters. The flowers may be red, pink, purple, white or pale green. Nicki Series has fragrant blooms in many colors, and the flowers stay open all day. The compact plants grow up to 18" tall.

'Only the Lonely' grows up to 4' tall and bears white blooms that are scented in the evening. **Sensation Series** plants grow up to 30" tall and bear red, white or pink flowers that stay open all day.

*N. sylvestris* grows up to 4' tall and bears white blooms that give off a scent in the evening.

## Problems & Pests

Tobacco mosaic virus, aphids, white-flies and downy or powdery mildew may cause occasional problems.

*N.* x *sanderae* (above)

Nicotiana *was named for Jean Nicot (1530–1600), a French consul in Portugal. He is credited with introducing this New World genus to France.*

N. tabacum *is the plant used for cigarette tobacco; it is, in a sense, the deadliest plant in the world.*

*N. sylvestris* & Nicki Series (right)

# Painted-Tongue
## Velvet Flower
*Salpiglossis*

**Height:** up to 24"  **Spread:** 12"  **Flower color:** red, yellow, orange, pink, purple; often patterned bicolors

'VIVID' IS THE WORD TO DESCRIBE THIS RELATIVELY LITTLE KNOWN and underused annual. The flowers are deeply colored and accented with contrasting throats. Unfortunately this beauty is somewhat ephemeral, as the stems are easily mashed down or broken. Place painted-tongue where it can be supported by other plants and where it is protected from the elements. And if it does succumb, take out your garden shears and create a lovely floral centerpiece.

## Planting

**Seeding:** Indoors in late winter; direct sow in spring

**Planting out:** After last frost

**Spacing:** 12"

## Growing

Painted-tongue prefers **full sun** but tolerates light shade. The soil should be **fertile,** rich in **organic matter** and **well drained.** A location sheltered from heavy rain and wind will keep these plants looking their best.

As with many members of the potato/tomato family, the seeds of painted-tongue are very tiny and shouldn't be covered with soil. They will germinate more evenly if kept in darkness until they sprout—place pots in a dark closet or cover pots with dark plastic or layers of newspaper. Once they start to sprout, the plants can be moved to a well-lit location.

## Tips

Painted-tongue is useful in the middle or back of beds and borders. It can also be added to large mixed containers. Most types of painted-tongue can become battered in rain and wind, so plant in a warm, sheltered area of the garden.

## Recommended

*S. sinuata* is an upright species in the same family as petunias. '**Blue Peacock**' has blue flowers with yellow throats and dark veins. Plants of the **Casino Series,** with flowers in a wide range of colors, bloom early and tolerate rain and wind. **Royale Series** has flowers with more pronounced veining in the throat.

## Problems & Pests

Occasional problems with aphids or root rot are possible.

*The iridescent quality of these flowers causes their color to change as they turn in a breeze.*

# Passion Flower

*Passiflora*

**Height:** up to 30'  **Spread:** variable  **Flower color:** white or pale pink petals with blue or purple bands

PASSION FLOWERS ARE EXOTIC AND MESMERIZING. THEY ARE sometimes included in Bible gardens because they are said to symbolize the Passion of Christ. Some biblical scholars say that because most passion flowers are native to North America, and not the Mediterranean or Middle East, they do not belong in a Bible garden. In any event, these intricate plants are beautiful. Most species are not hardy in Ohio. One that will survive a Zone 5 or 6 winter is the maypop *(P. incarnata)*. But beware—it may take over your garden. It dies back to the ground in cold winters and emerges in May ready to grow 10–25' in one season.

## Planting

**Seeding:** Not recommended

**Planting out:** Several weeks after last frost

**Spacing:** 12"

## Growing

Grow passion flower in **full sun** or **partial shade**. This plant prefers **well-drained, moist** soil of **average** fertility. Keep it **sheltered** from wind and cold.

Germination is erratic and propagation is generally easier from cuttings, but for gardeners who like a challenge, it is possible to propagate passion flower from seed. Soak seeds for 24 hours in hot water before planting. Place the seed tray in full sun because the seeds need light to germinate. Keep the soil moist and at about 59° F.

## Tips

Passion flower is a popular addition to mixed containers and makes an unusual focal point near a door or other entryway. This plant is actually a fast-growing woody climber that is grown as an annual.

Many garden centers now sell small passion flower plants in spring, which quickly climb trellises and other supports over summer. They can be composted at the end of summer or cut back and brought inside to enjoy in a bright room over winter.

The small round fruits are edible but not very tasty.

## Recommended

*P. caerulea* (blue passion flower) bears unusual purple-banded, purple-white flowers all summer. '**Constance Elliott**' bears fragrant, white flowers.

*P. incarnata* (maypop) has flowers that are pale lavender with an undertone of green. It is native to the southeastern U.S. and is root hardy in Ohio.

## Problems & Pests

Spider mites, whiteflies, scale insects and nematodes may cause occasional trouble.

*The common name refers not to physical love but to Christ's Passion. The three stigmas of the flower are said to represent the nails and the five anthers the wounds.*

# Periwinkle
## Madagascar Periwinkle
### *Catharanthus*

**Height:** 12–24"  **Spread:** usually equal to or greater than height  **Flower color:** red, rose, pink, mauve, apricot or white, often with contrasting centers

PERIWINKLE CONTAINS POWERFUL ALKALOIDS THAT ARE USED in the treatment of a variety of cancers. It is planted in the herb garden at Inniswood Metro Gardens every year. Because it looks so unassuming in the front of the garden at the feet of yarrow and other medicinal herbs, many visitors are surprised that this petite, charming plant is so powerful. Plants hold many secrets that we have yet to discover.

## Planting

**Seeding:** Indoors in mid-winter

**Planting out:** After last frost

**Spacing:** 8–18"

## Growing

Periwinkle prefers **full sun** but tolerates partial shade. Any **well-drained** soil is fine. This plant tolerates pollution and drought but prefers to be watered regularly. It doesn't like to be too wet or too cold. Avoid planting periwinkle until the soil has warmed because it may fail to thrive if planted in cold or wet soil.

Keep seedlings warm and take care not to overwater them. The soil temperature should be 55°–64° F for seeds to germinate.

*C. roseus*

## Tips

Periwinkle will do well in the sunniest, warmest part of the garden. Plant it in a bed along an exposed driveway or against the south-facing wall of the house. It can also be used in hanging baskets, in planters and as a temporary groundcover.

This plant is a perennial that is grown as an annual. In a bright room, it can be grown as a houseplant.

## Recommended

*C. roseus* (*Vinca rosea*) forms a mound of strong stems. The flowers are pink, red or white, often with contrasting centers. '**Apricot Delight**' bears pale apricot flowers with bright raspberry red centers. **Cooler Series** plants have light-colored flowers with darker, contrasting centers. '**Pacifica**' has flowers in various colors on compact plants.

## Problems & Pests

Slugs can be troublesome. Most rot and other fungal problems can be avoided by not overwatering.

*One of the best annuals to use in front of homes on busy streets, periwinkle will bloom happily despite exposure to exhaust fumes and dust.*

# Persian Shield

*Strobilanthes*

**Height:** 18–36" **Spread:** 24–36" **Flower color:** blue; plant grown for green, purple and silver foliage

WITH PERSIAN SHIELD'S IRIDESCENT FOLIAGE, WHO NEEDS FLOWERS? This tropical shrub from Burma adds a cool, shimmery touch to the front of a sunny bed or to a large container planting. Persian shield is a perfect foil for the brighter colors of the tropical plants that are so much in vogue. Imagine the electricity generated by the combination of Persian shield with a yellow angel's trumpet (*Brugmansia* 'Charles Grimaldi').

## Planting

**Seeding:** Not recommended

**Planting out:** After last frost, in warm soil

**Spacing:** 24"

## Growing

Persian shield grows well in **full sun** and **partial shade**. The soil should be **average to fertile, light** and very **well drained**. Pinch growing tips to encourage bushiness or the plant will tend to be lanky.

## Tips

The colorful foliage provides a dramatic background in annual or mixed borders and in container plantings. Combine with yellow- or white-flowered plants for a stunning contrast.

Root cuttings or tip cuttings can be started in late summer if you'd like indoor plants for the winter.

## Recommended

*S. dyerianus* is a tender shrub that is grown as an annual. It forms a bushy mound of silver- or purple-flushed foliage with contrasting dark green or purple veins and margins. The foliage emerges purple and matures to silver. Plants may produce spikes of blue flowers in early fall.

## Problems & Pests

Trouble with root rot is possible in very wet soils.

# Petunia

*Petunia*

**Height:** 6–18"  **Spread:** 12–24" or more  **Flower color:** pink, purple, red, white, yellow, coral, blue or bicolored

PETUNIAS WERE SO COMMON WHEN I WAS A CHILD THAT I resolved they would *never* be in my garden. One should never say never: I have fallen in love with petunias in the Wave and Fantasy series. I tuck them into the spaces between plants at the front of the border. Here they create a bridge between the main flowering times of my perennials. They weather our hot humid summers well and will survive a light frost. Another favorite is a yellow grandiflora—'Prism Sunshine.' It is that shade of yellow that glows in the early evening light.

## Planting

**Seeding:** Indoors in mid-winter

**Planting out:** After last frost

**Spacing:** 12–18"

## Growing

Petunias prefer **full sun**. The soil should be of **average to rich fertility, light, sandy** and **well drained**. When sowing, press seeds into the soil surface but don't cover them with soil. Pinch halfway back in mid-summer to keep plants bushy and to encourage new growth and flowers.

## Tips

Use petunias in beds, borders, containers and hanging baskets.

## Recommended

*P.* x *hybrida* is a large group of popular, sun-loving annuals that fall into three categories: grandifloras, multifloras and millifloras.

Fantasy Series (above), grandiflora type (below)

*The name* Petunia *is derived from* petun, *the Brazilian word for tobacco, which comes from species of the related genus* Nicotiana.

Multiflora type (above), milliflora type (below)

The **grandiflora** petunias have the largest flowers—up to 4" across. They have the widest variety of colors and forms, but they are the most likely to be damaged by heavy rain. **Daddy Series** plants are available in darkly veined shades of pink and purple. '**Prism Sunshine**' is a 1998 All-America Selections winner. Its compact plants bear pale yellow flowers with deeper yellow throats. **Supercascade Series** come in a wide variety of colors. Cultivars in the **Ultra Series** are available in many colors, including bicolors, and recover quite quickly from weather damage.

Compared to the grandifloras, the **multiflora** petunias have smaller blooms (about half the size), bear many more flowers and tolerate adverse weather conditions better. **Carpet Series** plants are available in a wide variety of colors. '**Priscilla**' is an attractive mounding plant with pale mauve flowers with darker purple veining. Most of the flowers have a second ring of smaller ruffled petals in the center of the flower. **Surfinia Series** plants branch freely, are self-cleaning and form a neat mound covered by a mass of flowers in shades of pink, blue, purple and white. Look for new additions to the series, which feature double flowers, minis, pastel colors and decorative veining. **Wave Series** plants are available in pink, purple and coral. Their low, spreading habit makes these plants popular as groundcovers and for hanging baskets and containers. The plants recover well from rain damage, bloom nonstop, tolerate cold and spread quickly.

The **milliflora** petunias are the newest group. The flowers are about 1" across and are borne profusely over the whole plant. These plants tolerate wet weather very well and sometimes self-seed. They are popular in mixed containers and hanging baskets and are also very nice in garden beds, forming neat mounds of foliage and flowers. **Fantasy Series** has plants in shades of red, purple, pink and white, although the pinks tend to be easiest to find. With the growing popularity of the millifloras, more colors will likely become available.

## Problems & Pests

Aphids and fungi may present problems. Fungal problems can be avoided by wetting the foliage as little as possible and by providing a location with good drainage.

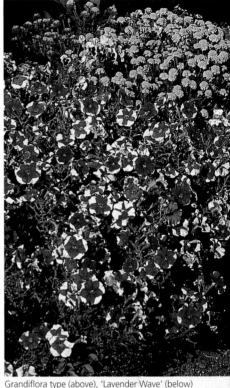

Grandiflora type (above), 'Lavender Wave' (below)

# Phlox

## Annual Phlox, Drummond's Phlox

*Phlox*

---

**Height:** 6–18"  **Spread:** 10" or more  **Flower color:** purple, pink, red, blue, white, yellow

AS IT IS WITH SO MANY TRUE ANNUALS, THE MAIN MISSION OF *Phlox drummondii* is to flower, set seed and then decline. It is imperative that you remove spent flowers in order to enjoy the beauty and fragrance of phlox throughout the season. Annual phlox presents a bit of a conundrum to the gardener. It prefers an evenly moist soil, but if the leaves are damp or the air is humid, fungal problems result. Avoid overhead irrigation and use a light mulch to preserve soil moisture. Combine annual phlox with other free-spirited plants such as poppies and tender sages.

## Planting

**Seeding:** Direct sow in early spring and mid-summer

**Spacing:** Up to 8"

## Growing

Phlox prefers **full sun**. The soil should be **fertile, moist** and **well drained**. This plant resents being transplanted, and starting it indoors is not recommended. Germination takes 10–15 days. Phlox can be propagated from cuttings and will root easily in moist soil. Plants can be spaced quite close together.

Deadhead to promote blooming.

## Tips

Use phlox on rock walls and in beds, borders, containers and rock gardens. To discourage disease, do not overwater and don't let the foliage stay wet at night.

## Recommended

*P. drummondii* forms a bushy plant that can be upright or spreading. It bears clusters of white, purple, pink or red flowers. **'Coral Reef'** bears attractive pastel-colored flowers. **Twinkle Mixed** has compact plants 8" tall that bear unusual star-shaped flowers. The colors of the petal margins and centers often contrast with the main petal color.

## Problems & Pests

To avoid fungal problems, provide good drainage and don't let water stand on the leaves late in the day. Water the plants in the morning during dry spells and avoid handling wet foliage.

*P. drummondii* (photos this page)

*This Texan species of* Phlox *is named for Thomas Drummond (1790–1835), who collected plants in North America.*

# Poppy
## Shirley Poppy, Corn Poppy, Flanders Poppy
*Papaver*

**Height:** 1–4'  **Spread:** 12"  **Flower color:** red, pink, white, purple, yellow, orange

POPPIES BRING TO MY MIND AN IMAGE FROM *THE WIZARD OF OZ* in which Dorothy and friends run through a field of deeply hued flowers. She and the Cowardly Lion slowly succumb to the sleep-inducing qualities of what appears to be the opium poppy. In real life it is not possible to fall asleep by simply smelling the flower. An extensive process is used to distill the narcotic compounds from the seedpods. But the Hollywood interpretation does look good on film. All the poppies have an attraction that is difficult to deny, and I freely admit that I am addicted to their fragile beauty.

## Planting

**Seeding:** Direct sow every two weeks in spring

**Spacing:** 12"

## Growing

Poppies grow best in **full sun**. The soil should be **fertile** and **sandy** with lots of **organic matter** mixed in. Good drainage is essential.

Do not start seeds indoors because transplanting is often unsuccessful. Mix the tiny seeds with fine sand for even sowing. Do not cover, as the seeds need light for germination. Deadhead to prolong blooms.

## Tips

Poppies work well in mixed borders where other plants are slow to fill in. Poppies will fill in empty spaces early in the season then die back over the summer, leaving room for other plants. They can also be used in rock gardens, and the cut flowers are popular for fresh arrangements.

*P. nudicaule* (photos this page)

*The seeds of both Shirley poppy and opium poppy can be used to flavor baked goods such as muffins, breads and bagels.*

'Peony Flowered' (above), *P. somniferum* (below)

Be careful when weeding around faded summer plants; you may accidentally pull up late-summer poppy seedlings.

## Recommended

*P. nudicaule* (Iceland poppy) is a short-lived perennial grown as an annual. It grows 12–18" tall and 12" wide. Red, orange, yellow, pink or white flowers appear in spring and early summer. This plant tends to self-seed, but it will gradually disappear from the garden if left to its own devices. **'Champagne Bubbles'** bears flowers in solid and bicolored shades of red, orange and yellow.

*P. rhoeas* (Flanders poppy, field poppy, corn poppy) forms a basal rosette of foliage above which the flowers are borne on long stems. **'Mother of Pearl'** bears flowers in pastel pinks and purples. **Shirley Series** (Shirley poppy) has flowers in many colors. The flowers are single, semi-double or double with silky, cup-shaped petals.

*P. somniferum* (opium poppy) grows up to 4' tall. The flowers are red, pink, white or purple. This plant has a mixed reputation. Its milky sap is the source of several drugs, including codeine, morphine and opium. All parts of the plant can cause stomach upset and even coma except for the seeds, which are a popular culinary additive (poppy seeds). The seeds contain only minute amounts of the chemicals that make this plant pharmaceutically valuable. The large seed capsules are also dried and used in floral arrangements. Though propagation of the species is restricted in many countries, several attractive cultivars have been developed for ornamental use. '**Danebrog Lace**' originated in the 19th century. The single flowers have frilly red petals with a large white patch at the base of each petal. '**Peony Flowered**' has large, frilly double flowers in a variety of colors on plants that grow up to 36" tall.

*P. nudicaule* (above), Shirley Series (below)

## Problems & Pests

Poppies rarely have problems, although fungi may be troublesome if the soil is wet and poorly drained.

*For cut flowers, seal the cut end of each stem with a flame or boiling water.*

# Sage

*Salvia*

**Height:** 1–4'  **Spread:** 8"–4'  **Flower color:** red, blue, purple, burgundy, pink, orange, salmon, yellow, cream, white or bicolored

MY LOVE AFFAIR WITH THE SAGES BEGAN WITH THE CULINARY species, common sage *(S. officinalis)* and pineapple sage *(S. elegans)*. I discovered that fruit salad was wonderfully enhanced with the addition of minced pineapple sage. Next came the biennials: silver sage *(S. argentea)* and clary sage *(S. sclarea)*. My clary sage was a gift in the form of seeds that came from Bulgaria. I now pass this gift along to other gardeners. Finally, I progressed to the many tender sages that are becoming increasingly available to gardeners. At one time I thought I might run out of sages to try, but with over 900 species, this love affair will last a long time.

## Planting

**Seeding:** Indoors in mid-winter; direct sow in spring

**Planting out:** After last frost

**Spacing:** 10"

## Growing

All salvias prefer **full sun** but tolerate light shade. The soil should be **moist, well drained** and of **average to rich fertility,** with lots of **organic matter.**

To keep plants producing flowers, water often and fertilize monthly. Remove spent flowers before they begin to turn brown.

## Tips

Salvias look good grouped in beds, borders and containers. The flowers are long lasting and make lovely cut flowers for arrangements.

*S. elegans* (above), *S. farinacea* & *S. splendens* (below)

## Recommended

*S. argentea* (silver sage) is grown for its large, fuzzy, silvery leaves. It grows up to 36" tall, spreads about 24" and bears small white or pink-tinged flowers. This plant is a biennial or short-lived perennial grown as an annual.

*S. coccinea* (Texas sage) is a bushy, upright plant that grows 24–36" tall and spreads about 12". It bears whorled spikes of white, blue or purple flowers. 'Coral Nymph' bears delicate pink flowers.

*S. elegans (S. rutilans;* pineapple sage) is a large, bushy plant with soft leaves and bright red flowers. It grows 3–4' tall, with an equal spread. The foliage smells of pineapple when crushed and is used as a culinary flavoring.

*S. splendens*

*S. farinacea* (mealy cup sage, blue sage) is a tender perennial that has bright blue flowers clustered along stems powdered with silver. The plant grows up to 24" tall, with a spread of 12". The flowers are also available in white. 'Victoria' is a popular cultivar with silvery foliage and deep blue flowers that make a beautiful addition to cut-flower arrangements.

*S. patens* (gentian sage) bears vivid blue flowers on plants 18–24" tall. This tender perennial is grown as an annual. Being tuberous-rooted, it can be lifted and brought inside for the winter in the same way as dahlias. 'Cambridge Blue' bears pale blue flowers.

*S. sclarea* (clary sage) is a biennial or short-lived perennial that grows to 30–36". In its second year this bold-textured plant produces large panicles of lilac to white flowers and self-seeds freely.

*S. splendens* (salvia, scarlet sage) is an annual that grows 12–18" tall and spreads up to 12". It is known for its spikes of bright red, tubular flowers. Recently, cultivars have become available in white, pink, purple and orange. 'Phoenix' forms neat, compact plants with flowers in many bright and pastel shades. 'Salsa' bears solid and bicolored flowers in shades of red, orange, purple, burgundy, cream and pink. Sizzler Series plants bear flowers in burgundy, lavender, pink, plum, red, salmon, and bicolored white and salmon. 'Vista' is an early-flowering, compact plant with dark blue-green foliage and bright red flowers.

*S. viridis (S. horminum;* annual clary sage) is grown for its colorful bracts, not its flowers. It grows 18–24" tall, with a spread of 8–12". **'Claryssa'** grows 18" tall and has bracts in pink, purple, blue or white. **'Oxford Blue'** bears purple-blue bracts.

## Problems & Pests

Seedlings are prone to damping off. Aphids and a few fungal problems may occur.

*The genus name* Salvia *comes from the Latin* salvus, *'save,' referring to the medicinal properties of several species.*

'Coral Nymph' (above), 'Victoria' (below)

# Scabiosa
## Pincushion Flower
### Scabiosa

**Height:** 18–36" **Spread:** up to 12" **Flower color:** purple, blue, maroon, pink, white, red

IN 1991 I PLANTED AN EVERLASTING GARDEN. I PURCHASED SEEDS and plants of flowers recommended for dried arrangements. My most successful everlastings were globe amaranth *(Gomphrena globosa)*, strawflowers *(Helichrysum* spp.), love-in-a-mist *(Nigella)*, winged everlasting *(Ammobium alatum)* and star flower *(Scabiosa stellata)*. It was an interesting garden, a carnival of colors in a somewhat jumbled array. The dried flowers and seedpods lasted for years and adorned many wreaths and vase arrangements.

### Planting
**Seeding:** Indoors in late winter; direct sow in mid-spring

**Planting out:** After last frost

**Spacing:** 12–16"

## Growing

Scabiosas grow best in **full sun**. The soil should be of **average to rich fertility, alkaline, well drained** and rich in **organic matter**. Keep soil moderately moist, but do not overwater.

## Tips

Scabiosas are useful in beds, borders and mixed containers. The flowers are also popular in fresh arrangements.

The tall stems of *S. atropurpurea* may fall over as the plants mature. Insert twiggy branches, called pea sticks, into the ground around the plants when they are small to give them support as they grow.

## Recommended

*S. atropurpurea* is an upright, branching plant growing up to 36" tall and spreading about 12". Its flowers may be white, blue, purple or red. **'Imperial Giants'** bears blooms in a deep maroon color and shades of pink. **Olympia Hybrids** bear flowers in a wide range of colors.

*S. stellata* (star flower) grows 18" tall and spreads half as much. This plant bears small white flowers but is grown for its papery seedpods, which dry in unusual globe shapes and are useful accents in dried arrangements. Pick *S. stellata* while still slightly green to keep the dried seedpods from shattering. **'Paper Moon'** ('Drumstick') bears blue flowers that dry to a warm bronze color.

*S. atropurpurea* (photos this page)

*The rounded, densely petaled blooms serve as a perfect landing pad for butterflies.*

# Snapdragon

*Antirrhinum*

**Height:** 6"–4' **Spread:** 6–24" **Flower color:** white, cream, yellow, orange, red, maroon, pink, purple or bicolored

WHAT CHILD HAS NOT MADE A SNAPDRAGON FLOWER talk? It is a natural puppet. For the uninitiated, gently grasp a flower by the sides at the joint of the 'lips' and carefully squeeze. Many members of the snapdragon (or figwort) family have flowers that look like mouths, and when they have upper and lower 'jaws,' we say that they are bilabiate, or two-lipped. We often give plants anthropomorphic or human qualities, especially if they look like they could talk. And, though plants can't talk, I know they are good listeners…

*Snapdragons may self-sow but the hybrids will not come true to type, so unless you enjoy experimenting you might wish to pull them out.*

## Planting

**Seeding:** Indoors in late winter; direct sow in spring

**Planting out:** After last frost

**Spacing:** 6–18"

## Growing

Snapdragons prefer **full sun** but tolerate light or partial shade. The soil should be **fertile**, rich in **organic matter** and **well drained**. These plants prefer a neutral or alkaline soil and will not perform as well in acidic soil. Do not cover seeds when sowing because they require light for germination.

To encourage bushy growth, pinch the tips of the young plants. Cut off the flower spikes as they fade to promote further blooming and to prevent the plant from dying back before the end of the season.

## Tips

The height of the variety dictates the best place for it in a border—the shortest varieties work well near the front, and the tallest look good in the center or back. The dwarf and medium-height varieties can also be used in planters, and there is even a trailing variety that does well in hanging baskets.

Snapdragons are perennials grown as annuals. They tolerate cold nights well into fall and may survive a mild winter. Self-sown seedlings may sprout the following spring if plants are left in place over winter, but because most snapdragons are hybrids, the seedlings will not come true to type.

## Recommended

There are many cultivars of *A. majus* available. Snapdragons are grouped into three size categories: dwarf, medium and giant.

**Dwarf** varieties grow up to 12" tall. 'Floral Showers' is a true dwarf, growing 6–8" tall. This plant bears flowers in a wide range of solid colors and bicolors. 'Lampion' is a new and interesting cultivar, usually grouped with the semi-dwarfs. It has a trailing habit and cascades up to 36", making it a great plant for hanging baskets. 'Princess' bears white-and-purple bicolored flowers. This plant produces many shoots from the base and therefore many flower spikes.

**Medium** snapdragons grow 12–24" tall. 'Black Prince' bears striking, dark purple-red flowers set against bronze-green foliage. **Sonnet Series** contains plants that grow to 36" tall and are just as attractive as cut flowers as they are in the garden.

**Giant** or **tall** cultivars can grow 3–4' tall. 'Madame Butterfly' has double flowers in a wide range of colors. The flowers of this cultivar are open-faced with a ruffled edge and they don't 'snap,' because the hinged, mouth-like structure has been lost with the addition of the extra petals. **Rocket Series** plants produce long spikes of brightly colored flowers. The flowers come in many shades and have good heat tolerance.

## Problems & Pests

Snapdragons can suffer from several fungal problems, including powdery mildew, fungal leaf spot, root rot, wilt and downy mildew. Snapdragon rust is the worst. To prevent rust, avoid wetting the foliage when watering, choose rust-resistant varieties and plant snapdragons in different parts of the garden each year. Aphids may also be troublesome.

*Snapdragons are interesting and long lasting in fresh flower arrangements. The buds will continue to mature and open even after the spike is cut from the plant.*

# Statice

*Limonium*

**Height:** 12–24" **Spread:** 6–12" **Flower color:** blue, purple, pink, white, yellow, red, orange

STATICE IS OFTEN USED IN FLOWER ARRANGEMENTS BECAUSE IT has a very long vase life. It is usually the last flower standing, lasting even longer than baby's breath. In the garden it offers a very long bloom time, especially if you cut it for fresh arrangements or for drying. Most of the flower colors hold true, although the red and orange selections tend to fade to pink and peach, respectively, as they dry. The peach color is very attractive when combined with dried grasses and seedpods for a subtle late-fall display.

*Statice, also known as sea lavender, is native to the Mediterranean and is adapted to dry, saline habitats.*

## Planting

**Seeding:** Indoors in mid-winter; direct sow in spring

**Planting out:** After last frost

**Spacing:** 6–12"

## Growing

Statice prefers **full sun**. The soil should be of **poor** or **average fertility, light, sandy** and **well drained**. Overly fertile soil causes statice to grow too tall and fall over. This plant doesn't like having its roots disturbed, so if starting it indoors, use peat pots. Germination takes 14–21 days.

## Tips

Statice makes an interesting addition to any sunny border, particularly in informal gardens. It is a perennial grown as an annual.

The basal leaves of statice form a rosette, and the flower stalk is sent up from the middle of the plant. Space the plants quite close together to make up for this lack of width.

*L. sinuatum*

*Statice is frequently grown in cutting gardens and can be used in fresh and dried arrangements.*

Cut statice for drying late in summer, before the white center has come out on the bloom. To dry statice, you can hang it upside down in a cool, dry place or simply stand the stalks in a vase with about 1" of water and they will dry quite nicely on their own as the water is used up.

## Recommended

*L. sinuatum* forms a basal rosette of hairy leaves. Ridged stems bear clusters of small, papery flowers in blue, purple, pink or white. '**Fortress**' has strongly branching plants and flowers in several bright and pastel shades. The plants grow up to 24" tall. **Petite Bouquet Series** has compact plants, 12" tall, with flowers in blue, purple, pink, white and yellow. '**Sunset**' grows 24" tall and bears flowers in warm red, orange, peach, yellow, apricot and salmon shades.

## Problems & Pests

Most problems can be avoided by providing a well-drained site and ensuring that there is good air circulation around the plants.

# Stock

## *Matthiola*

**Height:** 8–36" **Spread:** 12" **Flower color:** pink, purple, red, rose, yellow, white

STOCK HAS A HEADY SCENT THAT I WISH COULD BE BOTTLED. These plants are members of the mustard family and have that family's characteristic love of cooler temperatures. Place them in that sunny, airy spot in your garden. You will need to keep the soil evenly moist, but not wet, during the heat of summer. An option is to cut plants back in summer and hope they will start flowering again when cooler temperatures arrive in fall. I have grown stock, but twice I have had good growth in spring followed by sad plants in summer just as they were entering their main bloom. I now visit my local florist and buy stock to satisfy my yearning for its scent.

*When cutting stock flowers for arrange-ments, cut and then crush the woody stems so they will draw water more easily.*

## Planting

**Seeding:** Indoors in mid-winter; direct sow around last-frost date. Do not cover seeds because they require light to germinate.

**Planting out:** After last frost

**Spacing:** 12"

## Growing

Stock plants prefer **full sun** but tolerate partial shade. The soil should be of **average fertility**, have lots of **organic matter** worked in and be **moist** but **well drained**. Taller plants may need to be staked.

Shelter from the hot afternoon sun helps keep these plants looking good and blooming well.

A second sowing in mid-summer may result in fall blooms when the weather cools.

## Tips

Stocks can be used in mixed beds or in mass plantings.

Night-scented stock should be planted where its wonderful scent can be enjoyed in the evening—near windows that are left open, beside patios or along pathways. It is best to place night-scented stock with other plants because it tends to look wilted and bedraggled during the day but revives impressively at night.

## Recommended

*M. incana* (stock) has many cultivar groups. Its colors range from pink and purple to red, rose or white. The height can be 8–36", depending on the cultivar. The compact plants in **Cinderella Series** grow about 10" tall

Cinderella Series

and have fragrant, colorful flowers. The plants in **Excelsior Mammoth Column Series** grow about 36" tall and 12" wide. The flower spikes are up to 12" long and bear double flowers of red, pink, light purple, pale yellow or white.

*M. longipetala* subsp. *bicornis* (night-scented stock, evening-scented stock) has pink or purple flowers that fill the evening air with their scent. The plants grow 12–18" tall. '**Starlight Scentsation**' bears flowers in a wide range of colors.

## Problems & Pests

Root rot or other fungal problems may occur. Slugs may be attracted to young foliage.

# Strawflower
## Everlasting
*Xerochrysum (Bracteantha, Helichrysum)*

**Height:** 1–5' **Spread:** 12–24" **Flower color:** yellow, red, bronze, orange, pink, white, purple

THIS UNASSUMING AUSTRALIAN MEMBER OF THE DAISY FAMILY HAS flowers that are truly everlasting. I still have a small bowl filled with flower-heads from the early 1990s and they look as good as when I harvested them. The richly colored 'petals' are actually bracts, or modified leaves, that surround the minute flowers in the central disk. There are many decorative uses for strawflower. My son and I added some bracts to our homemade paper for an interesting effect. They also add a colorful note to potpourri.

## Planting

**Seeding:** Indoors in early spring; direct sow after last frost. Do not cover seeds because they require light to germinate.

**Planting out:** After last frost

**Spacing:** 10–18"

## Growing

Strawflower prefers locations that receive **full sun**. The soil should be of **poor to average fertility, neutral to alkaline, sandy, moist** and **well drained**. Strawflower is drought tolerant. Overwatering will cause the leaves to turn yellow and encourages disease. Overly fertile soil will cause the plants to grow too tall and flop over.

## Tips

Include strawflower in mixed beds, borders and containers. The lowest-growing varieties make useful edging plants. Taller varieties may require staking.

Strawflower is most often used for fresh or dried flower arrangements.

## Recommended

*X. bracteatum* (*Helichrysum bracteatum, Bracteantha bracteata*) is a tall, upright plant with gray-green foliage and brightly colored, papery flowers. The species can grow up to 5' tall, but the cultivars are generally a bit more compact. **Bright Bikini Series** has compact plants that grow to about 12" tall and bear large, colorful flowers. **'Golden Beauty'** is a Proven Winners selection. It bears bright yellow flowers and is useful in containers, hanging baskets and

window boxes. **Pastel Mixed** has smaller flowers in soft tones that blend well with other colors.

## Problems & Pests

Strawflower is susceptible to downy mildew.

*X. bracteatum* cultivars (photos this page)

# Sunflower

*Helianthus*

**Height:** dwarf varieties 24–36"; giants up to 15'  **Spread:** 12–24"
**Flower color:** most commonly yellow but also orange, red, brown, cream or bicolored; typically with brown, purple or rusty red centers

THERE ARE SO MANY SUNFLOWER OPTIONS, AND I HAVE NEVER seen one I didn't like. When our children were small, I planted the cultivar 'Mammoth.' They watched the plants grow and began calling them the Jack-in-the-beanstalk plants. Then as the seeds began to ripen, one by one, some midnight marauder began knocking down the plants and stealing the seeds, and often the whole seedhead. Our mystery was solved when we spied raccoon tracks around the plants. We never caught the perpetrators, but I'm sure they went into their winter sleep fat and happy.

## Planting

**Seeding:** Indoors in late winter; direct sow in spring

**Planting out:** After last frost

**Spacing:** 12–24"

## Growing

Sunflower grows best in **full sun.**
The soil should be of **average fertility, humus rich, moist** and **well drained.**

The annual sunflower is an excellent plant for children to grow. The seeds are big and easy to handle, and they germinate quickly. The plants grow continually upwards, and their progress can be measured until the flower finally appears at the top of the tall plant. If planted along the wall of a two-story house, beneath an upstairs window, the progress can be observed from above as well as below, and the flowers will be easier to see.

## Tips

The lower-growing varieties can be used in beds and borders. The tall varieties are effective at the backs of borders and make good screens and temporary hedges. The tallest varieties may need staking.

Birds will flock to the ripening seedheads of your sunflowers, quickly plucking out the tightly packed seeds. If you plan to keep the seeds to eat, you may need to place a mesh net, the sort used to keep birds out of cherry trees, around the flowerheads until the seeds ripen. The net can be a nuisance and doesn't look too nice; most gardeners leave the flowers to the birds and buy seeds for eating.

## Recommended

*H. annuus* (common sunflower) is considered weedy, but many new cultivars have been developed. '**Music Box**' is a branching plant that grows about 30" tall and has flowers in all colors, including some bicolors. '**Prado Red**' bears deep mahogany flowers and grows up to 5'. '**Russian Giant**' grows up to 10' tall and bears yellow flowers and large seeds. '**Teddy Bear**' has fuzzy-looking double flowers on compact plants 24–36" tall. This selection produces few, if any, seeds. '**Valentine**' bears creamy yellow flowers and grows up to 5'. '**Velvet Queen**' is a branching cultivar that bears many crimson red flowers.

## Problems & Pests

Powdery mildew may affect these plants.

*H. annuus* (above), 'Teddy Bear' (below)

# Swan River Daisy

*Brachyscome (Brachycome)*

**Height:** 8–18"  **Spread:** equal to or slightly greater than height
**Flower color:** blue, pink, white, purple; usually with yellow centers

THIS DELICATE DAISY IS A BIT PARTICULAR ABOUT ITS GROWING conditions. I prefer to use it in container plantings where I can control the soil moisture and sun orientation if necessary. During the spring, Swan River daisy gracefully falls over the front of the container. When the summer heat hits, I cut back the plant and turn the container around and let other plants, such as million bells, take center stage. In the cooler days of fall, Swan River daisy will once again turn on the charm and share the limelight with the other matured plants in the container.

*This Australian plant takes its name from the Swan, a river in southwestern Australia.*

## Planting

**Seeding:** Indoors in late winter; direct sow in mid-spring

**Planting out:** Early spring

**Spacing:** 12"

## Growing

Swan River daisy prefers **full sun** but benefits from light shade in the afternoon. The soil should be **fertile** and **well drained**. The soil should never be waterlogged, but if mature plants dry out, they will decline rapidly.

Plant out early because cool spring weather encourages compact, sturdy growth. This plant is frost tolerant and tends to die back when the summer gets too hot. Cut it back if it begins to fade, and don't plant it in hot areas of the garden.

## Tips

Use this versatile plant for edging beds and in rock gardens, mixed containers and hanging baskets.

Combine Swan River daisy with plants that mature later in the season. As Swan River daisy fades in July, the companions will be filling in and beginning to flower.

## Recommended

*B. iberidifolia* forms a bushy, spreading mound of feathery foliage. Blue-purple or pink-purple flowers are borne all summer. '**Bravo**' bears white, blue, purple or pink flowers profusely in a cool but bright spot. **Splendor Series** has dark-centered flowers in pink, purple or white.

## Problems & Pests

Aphids, slugs and snails cause occasional trouble for this plant.

# Sweet Pea

*Lathyrus*

**Height:** 1–6'  **Spread:** 6–12"  **Flower color:** pink, red, purple, blue, salmon, pale yellow, peach, white or bicolored

FRAGRANCE BRINGS MEMORIES AND ASSOCIATIONS TO MIND. When I smell fragrant sweet peas, I'm young again. I grew up in a neighborhood with a lot of children and a lot of chain-link fences that defined yards. Many neighbors used the vigorous sweet pea to adorn these utilitarian fences. It was easy to grow, pleasant to look at and delightful to smell.

*Sweet pea blossoms make attractive, long-lasting cut flowers. Cutting the flowers encourages still more blooms.*

## Planting

**Seeding:** Direct sow in early spring

**Spacing:** 6–12"

## Growing

Sweet pea prefers **full sun** but tolerates light shade. The soil should be **fertile,** high in **organic matter, moist** and **well drained.** Fertilize very lightly with a low-nitrogen fertilizer during the flowering season. This plant will tolerate light frost. Remove all spent blooms.

Soak seeds in water for 24 hours or nick them with a nail file before planting them. Planting a second crop of sweet pea about a month after the first one will ensure a longer blooming period.

## Tips

Sweet pea will grow up poles, trellises and fences or over rocks. The low-growing varieties form low, shrubby mounds. Grow sweet pea up a chain-link fence to hide the fence and provide privacy. The low-growing cultivars are also useful in planters and hanging baskets.

To help prevent diseases from afflicting your sweet pea plants, avoid planting in the same location two years in a row.

## Recommended

Many cultivars of *L. odoratus* are available. **Bijou Series** contains popular heat-resistant varieties that grow 18" tall, with an equal spread. Plants in this series need no support to grow. **Bouquet Mixed** is a tall, climbing variety. '**Cupid**' is a dwarf cultivar with fragrant, light

pink-and-white bicolored flowers. '**Painted Lady**' has very fragrant flowers that are deep pink and white bicolored. **Supersnoop Series** are sturdy bush types that need no support. Pinch the tips of the long stems to encourage low growth. The flowers are fragrant.

## Problems & Pests

Slugs and snails may eat the foliage of young plants. Root rot, mildew, rust and leaf spot may also afflict sweet pea occasionally.

# Verbena
## Garden Verbena
*Verbena*

**Height:** 8"–5'  **Spread:** 12–36"  **Flower color:** red, pink, purple, blue, yellow, scarlet, silver, peach or white; usually with white centers

BUTTERFLY WATCHING IS A PASSION OF MINE, AND VERBENAS offer butterflies a banquet. Butterflies prefer to light on a flat surface or the edges of a flat area to partake of their meals. *Verbena bonariensis* provides a perfect landing platform for a tiger swallowtail. The color contrast of this yellow and black butterfly with the magenta blooms of the verbena is stunning. Other butterfly visitors include silver-spotted skippers, great spangled fritillaries and painted ladies. The lower-growing verbenas attract their share of these flying jewels. Even the common cabbage white butterfly becomes iridescent when sitting on a 'Homestead Purple' verbena.

*If plants become leggy or overgrown, cut them back by one-half to tidy them up and promote lots of fall blooms.*

## Planting

**Seeding:** Indoors in mid-winter

**Planting out:** After last frost

**Spacing:** 18"

## Growing

Verbenas grow best in **full sun.** The soil should be **fertile** and very **well drained.** Pinch back young plants for bushy growth.

Chill seeds one week before sowing. Moisten the soil before sowing seeds. Do not cover the seeds with soil. Place the entire seed tray or pot in darkness, and water only if the soil becomes very dry. Once the seeds germinate, move them into the light.

## Tips

Use verbenas on rock walls and in beds, borders, rock gardens, containers, hanging baskets and window boxes. They make good substitutes for ivy-leaved geranium where the sun is hot and where a roof overhang keeps the mildew-prone verbenas dry.

*V.* x *hybrida* cultivars (photos this page)

*Verbenas need lots of sunlight in order to flower abundantly and stay free of fungal disease.*

*V. bonariensis* (above), *V. canadensis* (below)

## Recommended

*V. bonariensis* forms a low clump of foliage from which tall, stiff flower-bearing stems emerge. The small purple flowers are held in clusters. This plant grows up to 5' tall but spreads only 18–24". This species is a tender perennial grown as an annual that readily self-seeds.

*V. canadensis* (clump verbena, rose vervain) is a low-growing, spreading tender perennial native to south-central and southeastern North America. It grows up to 18" tall and spreads up to 36". It bears clusters of pink flowers from mid-summer to fall and is hardy to Zone 7, so it may survive a mild winter. '**Homestead Purple**' is the most common cultivar, more commonly grown in gardens than the species. It bears dark purple flowers all summer. This cultivar is mildew resistant. Other cultivars include '**Babylon**,' with light blue, lilac, magenta, pink, silver or white flowers, and '**Tukana**,' with flowers in shades of blue, salmon and scarlet.

*V.* x *hybrida* is a bushy plant that may be upright or spreading. It is a tender perennial grown as an annual. It bears clusters of small flowers in shades of white, purple, blue, pink, red or yellow. '**Peaches and Cream**' is a spreading plant with flowers that open to a soft peach color and fade to white. **Romance Series** has plants growing to 8–10" tall and bearing red, pink, purple or white flowers, with white eyes. '**Showtime**' bears brightly colored flowers on compact plants that grow to 10" tall and spread 18". Flowers in the **Temari Series** come in a range of colors. They are mildew resistant and heat tolerant with vigorous, spreading growth.

## Problems & Pests

Aphids, whiteflies, slugs and snails may be troublesome. Avoid fungal problems by ensuring good air circulation around the plants.

*The Romans, it is said, believed verbena could rekindle the flames of dying love. They named it* Herba Veneris, *'plant of Venus.'*

*V.* x *hybrida* cultivar (above), *V. bonariensis* (below)

# Viola
## Pansy, Johnny-Jump-Up
*Viola*

**Height:** 3–10"  **Spread:** 6–12"  **Flower color:** blue, purple, red, orange, yellow, pink, white, multi-colored

I LIKE TO USE PLANTS IN MY GARDEN THAT HAVE THE NAMES OF our children. For Sarah I found a dianthus, for Robert there is a geranium, and for John there are Johnny-jump-ups. Every year I plant groupings of *Viola tricolor* around the garden. Often I discover several seedlings from last year's plants. At Ohio State University many viola and pansy cultivars were studied for their hardiness and ornamental qualities. One of the recommendations that came out of the study was to plant violas and pansies in September for a beautiful spring show. Because of their preference for cooler temperatures, this strategy works beautifully.

*Johnny-jump-up is so named because it reseeds profusely and tends to show up in the most unlikely places. This small plant has an affinity for lawns and just about any nook or cranny it can find to grow in.*

## Planting

**Seeding:** Indoors in early winter or mid-summer

**Planting out:** Early spring or early fall

**Spacing:** 6"

## Growing

Violas prefer **full sun** but tolerate partial shade. The soil should be **fertile, moist** and **well drained**.

Violas do best when the weather is cool. They may die back completely in summer. Plants may rejuvenate in fall, but it is often easier to plant new ones in fall and not take up summer garden space with plants that don't look their best.

*V.* x *wittrockiana* cultivars (photos this page)

Direct sowing is not recommended. Sow seeds indoors in early winter for spring flowers and in mid-summer for fall and early-winter blooms. More seeds will germinate if they are kept in darkness until they sprout. Place seed trays in a dark closet or cover with dark plastic or layers of newspaper to block out the light.

*Viola flowers are edible and make delightful garnishes on salads and desserts. Make candied violets by brushing the flowers with whipped egg white and sprinkling them with super-fine sugar. Allow them to dry overnight.*

## Tips

Violas can be used in beds and borders, and they are popular for mixing in with spring-flowering bulbs. They can also be grown in containers. The large-flowered violas are preferred for early-spring color among primroses in garden beds.

## Recommended

*V. cornuta* (horned violet, viola) is low-growing, about 6" tall and 12–16" wide. The flowers are smaller than pansies and larger than Johnny-jump-ups, usually in shades of blue, purple or white with the distinctive and charming 'face' pattern violas are known for. **'Bambini'** produces flowers in a wider range of colors including shades of pink, yellow, orange, blue, purple and white. **Sorbet Series** is popular for the plants' wide color range and their cold tolerance. Planted in fall, they will flower until the ground freezes and may surprise you with another

show in spring. **'Sorbet Yesterday, Today and Tomorrow'** bears flowers that open white and gradually turn purple as they mature.

*V. tricolor* (Johnny-jump-up) is a popular species. The flowers are purple, white and yellow, usually in combination, although several varieties have flowers in a single color, often purple. This plant will thrive in gravel. **'Bowles Black'** has dark purple flowers that appear almost black. The center of each flower is yellow. **'Helen Mound'** ('Helen Mount') bears large flowers in the traditional purple, yellow and white combination.

*V. x wittrockiana* (pansy) comes in blue, purple, red, orange, yellow, pink and white, often multi-colored or with face-like markings. **'Floral Dance'** is popular for spring and fall displays as it is quite cold hardy; it

*V. tricolor*

has flowers in a variety of solid colors and multi-colors. **Imperial Series** includes plants that bear large flowers in a range of unique colors. **'Imperial Frosty Rose'** has flowers with deep rose pink centers that gradually pale to white near the edges of the petals. **Joker Series** has bicolored or multi-colored flowers with distinctive face markings. The flowers come in all colors. **'Maxim Marina'** bears light blue flowers with white-rimmed, dark blue blotches at the center. This cultivar tolerates both hot and cold temperatures. **Watercolor Series** is a newer group of cultivars with flowers in delicate pastel shades.

*V.* x *wittrockiana* cultivars (above & below), with tulips (below)

## Problems & Pests

Slugs and snails can be problems. Fungal problems can be avoided through good air circulation and good drainage.

*Collect short vases, such as perfume bottles with narrow necks, for displaying the cut flowers of violas. The more you pick, the more profusely the plants will bloom. These flowers are also among the easiest to press between sheets of wax paper, weighted down with stacks of books.*

# Wishbone Flower
## Blue Wings
*Torenia*

**Height:** 6–12" **Spread:** 6–12" **Flower color:** purple, pink, blue, burgundy, white; often bicolored with a yellow spot on the lower petal

THERE IS A LIMITED PALATE OF COLORFUL ANNUALS FOR MOIST shade. Impatiens have ruled for years, and many gardeners have indicated that they would like some options. So it is surprising that wishbone flower isn't used more. It has become available in several deeply colored cultivars, and it is the perfect plant to point out to children, who are often intrigued by familiar shapes showing up in strange places. Look deeply into the flower and you will see how wishbone flower came by its name.

## Planting

**Seeding:** Indoors in late winter

**Planting out:** After last frost date

**Spacing:** About 8"

## Growing

Wishbone flower prefers **light shade** but tolerates partial and full shade. The soil should be **fertile, light, humus rich** and **moist**. This plant requires regular watering.

Don't cover seeds when planting; they require light to germinate.

## Tips

Wishbone flower can be massed in a shaded bed or border, used as an edging plant or added to mixed containers and hanging baskets. It makes a nice change in shade gardens if you are tired of using impatiens. Try wishbone flower near a water feature, where the soil may remain moist for extended periods.

## Recommended

*T. fournieri* is a bushy, rounded to upright plant. It grows up to 12" tall, with an equal or lesser spread. Its purple flowers have yellow throats. **Clown Series** features compact plants that grow 6–10" tall. The flowers may be purple, blue, pink or white. **Duchess Series** has compact plants, up to 6" tall, and bears larger flowers in a range of colors.

## Problems & Pests

Fungal problems can occur in overly wet soils. Moist but not soggy soils are ideal.

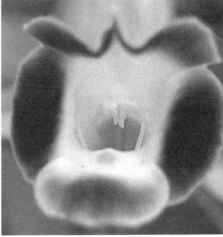

*T. fournieri* cultivar (above), *T. fournieri* (below)

*The stamens (male parts) in the center of the flower are arranged in the shape of a wishbone, giving rise to the common name.*

# Zinnia

*Zinnia*

**Height:** 6–36" **Spread:** 12" **Flower color:** red, yellow, green, purple, orange, pink, white, maroon, brown, gold

MANY IMPORTANT FOOD AND ORNAMENTAL PLANTS ARE NATIVE to the Americas. The culinary world gained corn, tomatoes, potatoes, chocolate and vanilla. The garden gained numerous members of the daisy family. Zinnias date back to the early 1500s when Spanish explorers found them growing in Montezuma's garden. More recently, zinnias have fallen into disfavor because of their susceptibility to several fungal diseases. Fortunately, cultivars have been selected that are resistant. A favorite is the Profusion Series. 'Profusion White' sparkles in the garden and in containers. And, best of all, zinnias seem to revel in our hot, dry summers.

## Planting

**Seeding:** Indoors in late winter; direct sow after last frost

**Planting out:** After last frost

**Spacing:** 6–12"

## Growing

Zinnias grow best in **full sun**. The soil should be **fertile**, rich in **organic matter, moist** and **well drained**. When starting seeds indoors, plant them in individual peat pots to avoid disturbing the roots when transplanting.

Deadhead zinnias to keep them flowering and looking their best. To keep mildew from the leaves and botrytis blight from the flowers, plant varieties that are resistant to these problems and avoid wetting the plants when you water.

'California Giants' (above), *Z. elegans* (below)

*Though zinnias are quite drought tolerant, they will grow best if watered thoroughly when the soil dries out. Use a soaker hose to avoid wetting the leaves.*

Z. haageana cultivar (above),
'California Giants' (below)

*The name* Zinnia *honors Johann Gottfried Zinn (1727–59), a German botany professor who first grew one of the South American zinnias from seed.*

## Tips

Zinnias are useful in beds, borders, containers and cutting gardens. The dwarf varieties can be used as edging plants. These plants are wonderful for fall color. Combine the rounded zinnia flowers with the spiky blooms of sun-loving salvia, or use the taller varieties in front of sunflowers.

## Recommended

*Z. angustifolia* (narrow-leaf zinnia) is a low, mounding plant that bears yellow and orange flowers. '**Crystal White**' bears white flowers on plants that grow 6–8" tall. It makes a wonderful edger for beds and borders.

*Z. elegans* and its cultivars bear flowers in several forms including single, double and cactus flowered, where the petals appear to be rolled into tubes like the spines of a cactus. '**California Giants**' are bushy plants growing to 36" and bearing large double flowers in a wide range of colors. '**Dreamland**' bears large double flowers up to 4" wide on plants about 10" tall. '**Peter Pan**' grows up to 12" tall, but it starts blooming early at 6", with flowers in mixed colors. **Thumbelina Series** has small flowers in all colors on dwarf, 6", weather-resistant plants.

*Z. haageana* (Mexican zinnia) is a bushy plant with narrow leaves. It grows 12–24" tall, spreads 12" and bears bright multi-colored, daisy-like flowers. This species is heat and drought tolerant and pest resistant. '**Persian Carpet**' bears bicolored and tricolored flowers in orange, red, yellow, maroon, brown and gold.

Z. **Profusion Series** includes fast-growing, mildew-resistant hybrids. The compact plants grow 10–18" tall and bear flowers in bright cherry red, orange or white; the individual cultivars are called '**Profusion Cherry**,' '**Profusion Orange**' and '**Profusion White**.'

## Problems & Pests

Zinnias are prone to mildew and other fungal problems. Prevent such problems by ensuring good air circulation and drainage.

'California Giants' (above), 'Profusion White' (below)

*Zinnias make excellent, long-lasting cut flowers for fresh arrangements.*

# OTHER ANNUALS TO CONSIDER

## Catch-Fly
*Silene*

Mediterranean native plants with attractive flowers in shades of pink and white. Self-seed; once established, may turn up in your garden every summer. *S. coeli-rosa* is upright, growing up to 20" tall and spreading 6". Has slender gray-green foliage and bright pink flowers, often with lighter pink or white centers. *S. pendula* is bushy, upright or spreading; grows 6–12" tall, with an equal spread. Bears loose clusters of nodding, single or double pink or white flowers. Grow in **full sun** or **light shade** with **fertile, moist, well-drained** soil. Both species are good filler plants in shrub and mixed borders, beds, planters and rock gardens.

## Cathedral Bells
*Cobaea scandens*

Vigorous climbing vine, native to Mexico. Can climb and spread 6–25' or more. Fragrant pale green or creamy white cup-shaped flowers darken to purple as they mature. Grow in **full sun** in a **sheltered** location with **average, moist, well-drained** soil. Too much nitrogen fertilizer encourages leafy growth but delays and reduces flowering. Provide a trellis, arbor or chain-link fence for plants to climb. Overwinter plants indoors, or take cuttings in late summer and root them to provide plants for the following summer.

## Chrysanthemum
*Chrysanthemum carinatum*

Upright plant with fleshy, finely divided foliage. Grows about 24" tall and spreads 12". Sometimes called painted daisy, a reference to the contrasting multi-colored bands on the petal bases. Both the Court Jesters and Rainbow Series cultivars have red, white, yellow and purple multi-colored, daisy-like flowers. Grow in **full sun** or **partial shade** with **average, well-drained** soil. Deadhead to prolong blooming. Several successive sowings will keep the colorful show going all summer. Attractive in informal beds, borders and planters; the blooms make good cut flowers. Sensitive people can develop a case of contact dermatitis after touching some chrysanthemums.

## Immortelle
*Xeranthemum annuum*

Upright plant with slen-
der-branched stems. Bears
single or semi-double
daisy-like flowers in
shades of purple, red, pink
or white. Grows about 24"
tall and spreads 18". Grow
in **full sun** in a **sheltered**
location with **average to
fertile, well-drained** soil.
Can be used in a bed, border or cutting garden;
flowers can be included in
fresh or dried arrange-
ments. Cut flowers before
they have completely
opened. Plants may need
support with twiggy
branches if a sheltered
location is not available.

## Mexican Mint
*Plectranthus*

Bushy plants that grow
8–12" tall and spread
about 36". *P. amionicus*
and *P. forsteri* are commonly available. Grow in
**light or partial shade** with
**fertile, moist, well-drained**
soil. These trailing plants
make fabulous fillers for
hanging baskets and
mixed containers. Plant
near a walkway or other
place where people will be
able to brush past the
plants and smell the spicy-
scented foliage. The plants
root easily from cuttings;
start some in late summer
to grow indoors through
winter.

## Mignonette
*Reseda odorata*

Bushy, upright plant,
growing 12–24" tall and
spreading 6–12". Incon-
spicuous flowers are red-
dish green and very
fragrant, attracting bees
and other pollen-loving
insects. Grow in **full sun**
or **partial shade** with **average to fertile, slightly alkaline, well-drained** soil.
Deadhead to prolong
flowering. Include
mignonette in a mixed
border with showier
plants. Place this fragrant
plant near a window, patio
or frequently used path-
way, so the scent can be
enjoyed.

282

# Quick Reference Chart
HEIGHT LEGEND: Low: < 12" • Medium: 12–24" • Tall: > 24"

| SPECIES by Common Name | White | Pink | Red | Orange | Yellow | Blue | Purple | Green | Foliage | Indoors | Direct | Low | Medium | Tall |
|---|---|---|---|---|---|---|---|---|---|---|---|---|---|---|
| Abutilon | • | • | • | • | • |  |  |  | • | • |  |  | • | • |
| African daisy | • | • | • | • | • |  |  |  |  | • | • |  | • |  |
| Ageratum | • | • |  |  |  | • | • |  |  | • | • | • | • | • |
| Alyssum | • | • |  |  | • |  | • |  |  | • | • | • |  |  |
| Amaranth |  |  | • |  | • |  |  | • | • | • | • |  |  | • |
| Anagallis | • | • | • |  |  | • |  |  |  | • |  | • | • |  |
| Angel's trumpet | • | • |  |  | • | • | • |  |  | • |  |  |  | • |
| Angelonia | • |  |  |  |  | • | • |  |  |  |  |  | • |  |
| Baby blue-eyes | • |  |  |  |  | • | • |  |  |  | • | • |  |  |
| Baby's breath | • | • |  |  |  |  | • |  |  | • | • | • | • |  |
| Bachelor's button | • | • | • |  |  | • | • |  |  | • | • |  | • | • |
| Bacopa | • |  |  |  |  | • |  | • |  |  |  | • |  |  |
| Begonia | • | • | • | • | • |  | • |  |  | • |  | • | • |  |
| Bells-of-Ireland |  |  |  |  |  |  |  | • |  | • | • |  |  | • |
| Bidens |  |  |  |  | • |  |  |  |  | • | • |  | • |  |
| Black-eyed Susan |  |  | • | • | • |  |  |  |  | • | • | • | • | • |
| Black-eyed Susan vine | • |  |  | • | • | • | • |  |  | • | • |  |  | • |
| Blanket flower |  |  | • | • | • |  |  |  |  | • | • |  | • | • |
| Blood flower | • |  | • | • | • |  |  | • |  | • |  |  |  | • |
| Browallia | • |  |  |  |  | • | • |  |  | • |  | • | • |  |
| Calendula | • |  |  | • | • |  |  |  |  |  | • | • | • |  |
| California poppy | • | • | • | • | • |  |  | • |  |  | • | • | • |  |
| Candytuft | • | • | • |  |  |  | • |  |  | • | • | • |  |  |
| Canterbury bells | • | • |  |  |  | • | • |  |  | • | • |  | • |  |
| Cape marigold | • | • |  | • | • |  |  |  |  | • | • |  | • |  |
| Celosia |  | • | • | • | • |  | • |  |  | • | • | • | • | • |
| Chilean glory flower |  |  | • | • |  |  |  |  |  | • |  |  |  | • |
| China aster | • | • | • |  | • | • | • |  |  | • | • | • | • | • |
| Chinese forget-me-not | • | • |  |  |  | • |  |  |  | • | • |  | • |  |
| Cleome | • | • |  |  |  |  | • |  |  | • | • |  | • | • |

# Quick Reference Chart

## SPECIES
### by Common Name

| Hardy | Half-hardy | Tender | Sun | Part Shade | Light Shade | Shade | Moist | Well Drained | Dry | Fertile | Average | Poor | Page Number | Species by Common Name |
|---|---|---|---|---|---|---|---|---|---|---|---|---|---|---|
| | | • | • | • | | | • | • | | • | • | | 48 | Abutilon |
| | | • | • | | | | • | • | | | • | | 50 | African daisy |
| | | • | • | • | | | • | • | | • | | | 52 | Ageratum |
| • | | | • | | • | | | • | | | • | • | 56 | Alyssum |
| | | • | • | | | | | • | | | • | • | 58 | Amaranth |
| • | • | | • | | | | • | • | | • | | | 62 | Anagallis |
| | | • | • | | | | • | • | | • | | | 64 | Angel's trumpet |
| | | • | • | • | | | • | | | • | | | 68 | Angelonia |
| • | | | • | • | | | • | • | | • | | | 70 | Baby blue-eyes |
| • | | | • | | | | | | • | | | • | 72 | Baby's breath |
| • | | | • | | | | • | • | | • | • | | 74 | Bachelor's button |
| | • | | | • | • | | • | | | | • | | 76 | Bacopa |
| | • | | | • | • | | | • | | • | | | 78 | Begonia |
| | • | | • | • | | | • | • | | • | • | | 82 | Bells-of-Ireland |
| | | • | • | | | | • | • | | • | • | | 84 | Bidens |
| | • | | • | • | | | • | • | • | • | | | 86 | Black-eyed Susan |
| | | • | • | • | • | | • | | | • | | | 90 | Black-eyed Susan vine |
| • | | | • | | | | | | • | | • | • | 92 | Blanket flower |
| | | • | • | | | | | • | • | • | • | | 94 | Blood flower |
| | | • | • | • | • | • | | • | | • | | | 96 | Browallia |
| • | | | • | • | | | | • | | | • | | 98 | Calendula |
| • | | | • | | | | | • | • | | • | • | 100 | California poppy |
| • | | | • | • | | | | • | | | • | • | 102 | Candytuft |
| • | | | • | • | | | • | | | • | | | 104 | Canterbury bells |
| | • | | • | | | | | • | • | • | | | 106 | Cape marigold |
| | • | | • | | | | • | • | | • | | | 108 | Celosia |
| | • | | • | | | | | • | | • | | | 112 | Chilean glory flower |
| | • | | • | • | | | • | • | | • | | | 114 | China aster |
| • | | | • | • | | | • | • | | | • | | 116 | Chinese forget-me-not |
| | • | | • | • | | | • | | • | | • | | 118 | Cleome |

# Quick Reference Chart
**HEIGHT LEGEND:** Low: < 12" • Medium: 12–24" • Tall: > 24"

| SPECIES by Common Name | COLOR | | | | | | | | | SOWING | | HEIGHT | | |
|---|---|---|---|---|---|---|---|---|---|---|---|---|---|---|
| | White | Pink | Red | Orange | Yellow | Blue | Purple | Green | Foliage | Indoors | Direct | Low | Medium | Tall |
| Climbing snapdragon | • | • | • | | | • | • | | | • | • | | • | • |
| Coleus | | | | | | | • | | • | • | | • | • | • |
| Coreopsis | | | • | • | • | | | | | • | • | • | | • |
| Cosmos | • | • | • | • | • | | | | | • | • | | • | • |
| Creeping zinnia | | | | • | • | | | | | | • | • | | |
| Cup flower | • | | | | | • | • | | | • | | • | | |
| Dahlberg daisy | | | | • | • | | | | | • | • | • | | |
| Dahlia | • | • | • | • | • | | • | | • | • | • | • | • | • |
| Diascia | | • | | | | | | | | • | | • | | |
| Dusty miller | • | | | | • | | | • | | • | | | • | |
| Dwarf morning glory | | • | | | | • | • | | | • | • | • | • | |
| Fan flower | | | | | | • | • | | | • | | • | | |
| Felicia | • | | | | | • | | | | • | • | • | | |
| Flowering flax | • | • | • | | | • | • | | | | • | | • | • |
| Four-o'clock flower | • | • | • | | • | | | | | • | • | | • | • |
| Fuchsia | • | • | • | • | | | • | | | | | • | • | • |
| Gazania | • | • | • | • | • | | | | | • | • | • | • | |
| Geranium | • | • | • | • | | | • | | • | • | | • | • | • |
| Globe amaranth | • | • | • | • | | | • | | | • | | • | • | • |
| Godetia | • | • | • | | | | • | | | • | | • | • | • |
| Heliotrope | • | | | | | • | • | | | • | | • | • | • |
| Hyacinth bean | • | | | | | | • | | | • | • | | | • |
| Impatiens | • | • | • | • | • | | • | | • | • | | • | • | • |
| Lantana | • | • | • | • | • | | • | | | • | | | • | |
| Larkspur | • | • | | | | • | • | | | • | • | | • | • |
| Lavatera | • | • | • | | | | • | | | • | • | | • | • |
| Licorice plant | • | | | | • | | | • | | | | • | • | |
| Lisianthus | • | • | | | | • | • | | | • | | • | • | • |
| Livingstone daisy | • | • | • | • | • | | • | | • | • | • | • | | |
| Lobelia | • | • | • | | | • | • | | | | | • | | |

# Quick Reference Chart

## SPECIES
### by Common Name

| Hardy | Half-hardy | Tender | Sun | Part Shade | Light Shade | Shade | Moist | Well Drained | Dry | Fertile | Average | Poor | Page Number | Species |
|---|---|---|---|---|---|---|---|---|---|---|---|---|---|---|
| | | • | • | • | • | | • | • | | • | • | | 122 | Climbing snapdragon |
| | | • | • | • | • | • | • | • | | • | • | | 124 | Coleus |
| • | | | • | | | | | • | • | • | • | | 128 | Coreopsis |
| | | • | • | | | | | • | • | | • | • | 130 | Cosmos |
| | | • | • | • | | | | • | • | | • | | 134 | Creeping zinnia |
| | • | | • | • | | | • | | | | • | | 136 | Cup flower |
| • | | | • | | | | | • | | | • | • | 138 | Dahlberg daisy |
| | | • | • | | | | • | • | | • | | | 140 | Dahlia |
| | • | | • | • | | | • | | | • | | | 144 | Diascia |
| | • | | • | | • | | | • | | | • | | 146 | Dusty miller |
| | | • | • | | | | | • | | | • | • | 148 | Dwarf morning glory |
| | | • | • | | • | | • | • | | | • | | 150 | Fan flower |
| | • | | • | | | | | • | | | • | | 152 | Felicia |
| • | | | • | • | | | | • | • | | • | | 154 | Flowering flax |
| | | • | • | • | | | • | • | • | • | | | 156 | Four-o'clock flower |
| | | • | | | • | • | • | • | | • | | | 158 | Fuchsia |
| | | • | • | | | | | • | • | | • | • | 162 | Gazania |
| | | • | • | • | | | | • | | • | | | 164 | Geranium |
| | | • | • | | | | | • | • | | • | | 168 | Globe amaranth |
| • | | | • | | • | | | • | • | | • | • | 170 | Godetia |
| | • | | • | | | | • | • | | • | | | 172 | Heliotrope |
| | • | | • | | | | • | • | | • | | | 176 | Hyacinth bean |
| | | • | • | • | • | • | • | • | | • | | | 178 | Impatiens |
| | • | | • | • | | | • | • | • | • | | | 182 | Lantana |
| • | | | • | | • | | • | • | | • | | | 184 | Larkspur |
| • | | | • | | | | • | | | | • | | 186 | Lavatera |
| | • | | • | | | | • | • | | | • | • | 190 | Licorice plant |
| | • | | • | • | • | | | • | | | • | | 192 | Lisianthus |
| | | • | • | | | | | • | • | | • | • | 194 | Livingstone daisy |
| • | | | | | • | • | • | | | | • | | 196 | Lobelia |

# Quick Reference Chart

HEIGHT LEGEND: Low: < 12" • Medium: 12–24" • Tall: > 24"

| SPECIES by Common Name | COLOR | | | | | | | | | SOWING | | HEIGHT | | |
|---|---|---|---|---|---|---|---|---|---|---|---|---|---|---|
| | White | Pink | Red | Orange | Yellow | Blue | Purple | Green | Foliage | Indoors | Direct | Low | Medium | Tall |
| Love-in-a-mist | • | • | | | | • | • | | • | • | • | | • | |
| Marigold | • | | • | • | • | | | | • | • | • | • | • | • |
| Mexican sunflower | | | • | • | • | | | | | • | • | | • | • |
| Million bells | • | • | • | • | • | • | • | | | | | • | | |
| Monkey flower | • | • | • | • | • | | • | | | • | | • | | |
| Morning glory | • | • | • | • | • | • | • | | • | • | • | | | • |
| Moss rose | • | • | • | • | • | | • | | | • | | • | | |
| Nasturtium | • | • | • | • | • | | • | | • | • | • | | • | |
| Nemesia | • | • | • | • | • | • | • | | | • | | • | • | |
| Nicotiana | • | • | • | | • | | • | • | | • | • | | • | • |
| Painted-tongue | | • | • | • | • | | • | | | • | • | • | • | |
| Passion flower | • | • | | | | • | • | | | • | | | | • |
| Periwinkle | • | • | • | | | | • | | | • | | | • | |
| Persian shield | | | | | | • | | | • | | | | • | • |
| Petunia | • | • | • | | • | • | • | | | • | | • | • | |
| Phlox | • | • | • | | • | • | • | | | | • | • | • | |
| Poppy | • | • | • | • | • | | • | | | | • | | • | • |
| Sage | • | • | • | • | • | • | • | | • | • | • | | • | • |
| Scabiosa | • | • | • | | | • | • | | | • | • | | • | • |
| Snapdragon | • | • | • | • | • | | • | | • | • | • | • | • | • |
| Statice | • | • | • | • | • | • | • | | | • | • | | • | |
| Stock | • | • | • | | • | | • | | | • | • | • | • | • |
| Strawflower | • | • | • | • | • | | • | | | • | • | | • | • |
| Sunflower | • | | • | • | • | | | | | • | • | | • | • |
| Swan river daisy | • | • | | | | • | • | | | • | • | • | • | |
| Sweet pea | • | • | • | | • | • | • | | | | • | | • | • |
| Verbena | • | • | • | | • | • | • | | | • | | • | • | • |
| Viola | • | • | • | • | • | | • | | | • | | • | | |
| Wishbone flower | • | • | | | | • | • | | | • | | • | | |
| Zinnia | • | • | • | • | • | | • | • | | • | • | • | • | • |

# Quick Reference Chart

| Hardy | Half-hardy | Tender | Sun | Part Shade | Light Shade | Shade | Moist | Well Drained | Dry | Fertile | Average | Poor | Page Number | SPECIES by Common Name |
|---|---|---|---|---|---|---|---|---|---|---|---|---|---|---|
| HARDINESS | | | LIGHT | | | | SOIL CONDITIONS | | | | | | | |
| • | | | • | | | | | • | | | • | | 198 | Love-in-a-mist |
| | • | | • | | | | | • | • | | • | | 200 | Marigold |
| | | • | • | | | | | • | • | | • | • | 204 | Mexican sunflower |
| | • | | • | | | | • | • | • | • | | | 206 | Million bells |
| | • | • | | • | • | | • | | | • | | | 208 | Monkey flower |
| | | • | • | | | | | • | | | • | • | 210 | Morning glory |
| | | • | • | | | | | | • | | | • | 214 | Moss rose |
| | | • | • | • | • | | • | • | • | | • | • | 216 | Nasturtium |
| | | • | • | | | | • | • | | • | • | | 220 | Nemesia |
| | | • | • | • | • | | • | | | • | | | 222 | Nicotiana |
| | | • | | | • | | | • | | • | | | 226 | Painted-tongue |
| • | | | • | • | | | • | • | | | • | | 228 | Passion flower |
| | | • | • | • | | | • | • | • | • | • | • | 230 | Periwinkle |
| | | • | • | • | | | | • | | | • | • | 232 | Persian shield |
| | • | | • | | | | | • | | | • | • | 234 | Petunia |
| • | | | • | | | | • | • | | • | | | 238 | Phlox |
| • | | | • | | | | | • | | • | | | 240 | Poppy |
| | • | • | • | | • | | • | • | | | • | • | 244 | Sage |
| | • | | • | | | | • | • | | | • | • | 248 | Scabiosa |
| | • | | • | • | • | | | • | | • | | | 250 | Snapdragon |
| | | • | • | | | | | • | | | • | • | 254 | Statice |
| • | | | • | • | | | • | | | | • | | 256 | Stock |
| | • | | • | | | | • | • | • | | • | • | 258 | Strawflower |
| • | | | • | | | | • | • | | | • | | 260 | Sunflower |
| | • | | • | • | | | | • | | • | | | 262 | Swan river daisy |
| • | | | • | | • | | • | • | | • | | | 264 | Sweet pea |
| • | | • | • | | | | | • | | • | | | 266 | Verbena |
| • | | | • | • | | | • | | | | • | | 270 | Viola |
| | | • | | • | • | • | • | | | • | | | 272 | Wishbone flower |
| | | • | • | | | | • | • | | • | | | 276 | Zinnia |

# GLOSSARY

**acid soil:** soil with a pH lower than 7.0

**alkaline soil:** soil with a pH higher than 7.0

**annual:** a plant that germinates, flowers, sets seed and dies in one growing season

**basal leaves:** leaves that form from the crown, at the base of the plant

**biennial:** a plant that germinates and produces stems, roots and leaves in the first growing season; it flowers, sets seed and dies in the second growing season

**crown:** the part of a plant at or just below soil level where the shoots join the roots

**cultivar:** a cultivated plant variety with one or more distinct differences from the species, e.g., in flower color, leaf variegation or disease resistance

**damping off:** fungal disease causing seedlings to rot at soil level and then topple over

**deadhead:** to remove spent flowers to maintain a neat appearance and encourage a longer blooming period

**desiccation:** drying out of plant tissue, especially foliage

**direct sow:** to sow seeds directly in the garden soil where the plants are to grow, as opposed to sowing first in pots or flats and transplanting

**disbud:** to remove some flowerbuds to improve the size or quality of the remaining ones

**dormancy:** a period of plant inactivity, usually during winter or unfavorable climatic conditions

**double flower:** a flower with an unusually large number of petals, often caused by mutation of the stamens into petals

**forma (f.):** a naturally occurring variant of a species; below the level of subspecies in biological classification and similar to variety

**genus:** a category of biological classification between the species and family levels; the first word in a scientific name indicates the genus

**half-hardy:** a plant capable of surviving the climatic conditions of a given region if protected from heavy frost or cold

**harden off:** to gradually acclimatize plants that have been growing in a protective environment (usually indoors) to a more harsh environment (usually outdoors in spring)

**hardy:** capable of surviving unfavorable conditions, such as cold weather or frost, without protection

**humus:** decomposed or decomposing organic material in the soil

**hybrid:** a plant resulting from natural or human-induced cross-breeding between varieties, species or genera; the hybrid expresses features of each parent plant

**lodging:** plants leaning or falling over

**neutral soil:** soil with a pH of 7.0

**node:** the area on a stem from which a leaf or new shoot grows

**pH:** a measure of acidity or alkalinity (the lower the pH, the higher the acidity); the pH of soil influences availability of nutrients for plants

**perennial:** a plant that takes three or more years to complete its life cycle; a herbaceous perennial normally dies back to the ground over winter

*potager:* a garden that combines function with beauty, often by growing vegetables, herbs and ornamental flowers together in a formal pattern of raised beds

**quilled:** the narrow, tubular shape of petals or florets of certain flowers

**rhizome:** a root-like food-storing stem that grows horizontally at or just below soil level, from which new shoots may emerge

**rootball:** the root mass and surrounding soil of a container-grown plant or a plant dug out of the ground

**runner:** a modified stem that grows on the soil surface; roots and new shoots are produced at nodes along its length

**semi-double flower:** a flower with petals that form two or three rings

**sepal:** segment of the outermost ring of a typical flower; usually green and leaf-like, but may be large, colorful and petal-like

**single flower:** a flower with a single ring of typically four or five petals

**species:** the fundamental unit of biological classification, simply defined as a group of interfertile organisms; the original entity from which cultivars and varieties are derived

**subshrub:** a plant that is somewhat shrubby or woody at the base; upper parts are herbaceous; tender subshrubs may be grown as annuals

**subspecies (subsp.):** a naturally occurring, regional form of a species, often isolated from other subspecies but still potentially interfertile with them

**taproot:** a root system consisting of one long main root with smaller roots branching from it

**tender:** incapable of surviving the climatic conditions of a given region and requiring protection from frost or cold

**tepal:** a sepal or petal of a flower, when the petals and sepals are not clearly distinguished from each other

**true:** the passing of desirable characteristics from the parent plant to seed-grown offspring; also called breeding true to type

**tuber:** the thick section of a rhizome bearing nodes and buds

**variegation:** foliage that has more than one color, often patched or striped or bearing differently colored leaf margins

**variety (var.):** a naturally occurring variant of a species; below the level of subspecies in biological classification

**xeriscape:** a landscaping method that conserves water by using native and drought-tolerant plants

# PLACES TO VISIT IN OHIO

## Garden to Visit

*Franklin Park has beautiful annual displays that change every year. Their displays are made up solely of annuals.*

Franklin Park Conservatory
1777 East Broad Street
Columbus, Ohio
(614) 645-TREE or (800) 214-PARK
http://www.fpconservatory.org

## Nurseries to Visit

ALEXANDRIA
Bakers Acres
3388 Castle Road
(740) 924-0500

CHAGRIN FALLS
Lowe's Greenhouses
16540 Chillicothe Road
(440) 543-5123
www.lowesgreenhouse.com

HOWARD
Homewood Farm
19520 Nunda Rd.
(740) 599-6638
www.homewoodfarm.com

STEWART
Glasshouse Works
Church St.
(740) 662-2142
www.glasshouseworks.com

WOOSTER
The Plant Patch
7374 Cleveland Rd
(330) 345-8658

# INDEX OF PLANT NAMES